Hitchcock with a Chinese Face

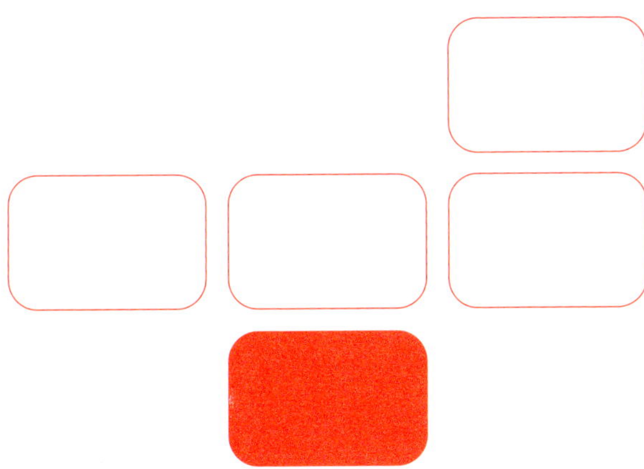

Hitchcock with a Chinese Face

Cinematic Doubles, Oedipal Triangles, and China's Moral Voice

JEROME SILBERGELD

University of Washington Press

Seattle and London

Hitchcock with a Chinese Face is published with generous support from the Publications Committee, Department of Art and Archaeology, Princeton University.

University of Washington Press
P.O. Box 50096, Seattle, WA 98145
www.washington.edu/uwpress

Library of Congress Cataloging-in-Publication Data

Silbergeld, Jerome.
    Hitchcock with a Chinese face : cinematic doubles, Oedipal triangles, and China's moral voice /
 Jerome Silbergeld.
       p.   cm.
    Includes bibliographical references and index.
    ISBN 0-295-98417-1 (alk. paper)
    1. Tian guo nie zi. 2. Suzhou He. 3. Hao nan hao nè. 4. Motion pictures—China—Foreign
 influences. 5. Motion pictures—Taiwan—Foreign influences. I. Title.

 PN1993.5.C4S825 2004
 791.43'75'0951—dc22   2004043095

The paper used in this publication meets the minimum requirements of American National Standard for Information Sciences—Permanence of Paper for Printed Library Materials, ANSI z39.48–1984.

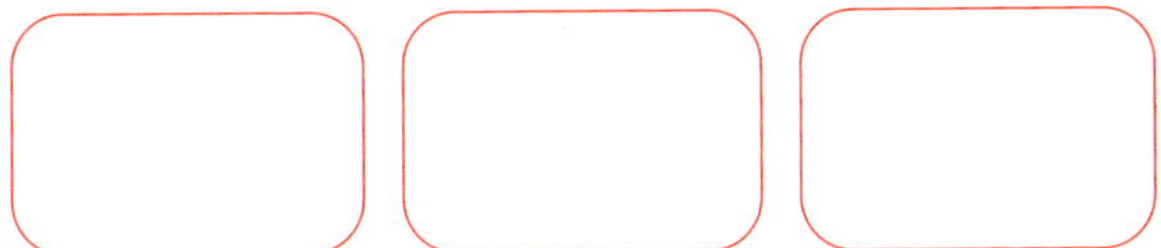

CONTENTS

DVD FILM SCENES

 *Suzhou River*

SCENE 1 The River

The unseen videographer introduces the audience to the seamy side of Shanghai and to his own hard-bitten realism. "There's a century worth of stories here and rubbish," he says. "The river will show you everything."

SCENE 2 Love, of Course

On her birthday, the young Mudan falls in love with her escort, the motorcycle courier Mada.

SCENE 3 "Am I the Mudan You're Looking For?"

After the "death" of Mudan, Mada visits the videographer's girlfriend and Mudan's look-alike, Meimei, in her dressing room.

SCENE 4 *Jietuo* / "Letting Go"

As Mada comes between them, Meimei and the videographer's relationship breaks up, set to the lyrics of the well-known song *Jietuo* ("breaking up" or "letting go") and a montage of the videographer's past work. An unidentified woman (perhaps a client of the videographer) mouths the music, wearing pigtails and looking ambiguously like an imitation of the young Mudan by the older Meimei, who is trading places with Mudan at this point. Both the music (made popular by Taiwanese superstar A-Mei) and the images describe the couple drifting apart, the videographer clinging to his photography and to the past, and Meimei letting go sadly but starting to adopt Mudan's innocent self-determination and preparing for the next stage of her life.

 *The Day the Sun Turned Cold*

SCENE 1 The Accusation

Guan Jian arrives at the police station to accuse his mother of having murdered his father ten years earlier and to face their disbelief.

SCENE 2 The Deathbed

Villagers gather around the stricken Guan Shichang's bed, suspicious of his wife Pu Fengying and her newfound male companion, recommending good old-fashioned measures to correct her behavior but failing to recognize the full gravity of the situation. Pu Fengying arrives to change Guan's medication—and perhaps to pollute it. Pu suddenly dashes out, sickened, leaving the dying father and son alone. Guan draws the tearful son Guan Jian close and instructs him never to reveal to others what he regards as the dreadful family secret.

SCENE 3   The Confrontation

Guan Jian returns home to directly confront Pu Fengying with his accusation.

Good Men, Good Women

SCENE 1   The Present, Haunted by the Past

In her apartment, awakened by the ringing of her fax machine, a hung-over and depressed actress Liang Ching reads pages sent by an anonymous caller from her stolen diary, detailing her sordid love affair with the murdered gangster Ah Wei. As she sings quietly to herself, "My heart is shattered. I just can't cope," the setting changes to the past, the lovers cavorting before a mirror.

SCENES 2 AND 3   "I Feel As If I'm Turning into Chiang Bi-Yu"

In China to perform the role of Taiwan's wartime patriot Chiang Bi-Yu, actress Liang Ching begins to identify with her as more than just a film subject. In a seamless transition, the fictional actress "becomes" the historical subject as Chiang Bi-Yu is interrogated by Chinese officers who suspect her of being a Japanese spy. Chiang's interrogation is followed by the scene of her husband Chung Hao-Tung's interrogation—the questioning punctuated by regional and language differences that emphasize the cultural separation of Taiwan from China. The noble subjects, Chiang and Chung, make a generational contrast with actress Liang Ching and her lover, as seen in the previous selection.

SCENE 4   The Death of Ah Wei

At a dance-hall meeting of rival underworld gangs, a drunk and probably drugged Liang Ching sings her own tragic song ("All around I see gilded lives / But mine is tarnished . . ."). As she dances with the ill-fated Ah Wei, he is shot to death in her arms.

SCENE 5   The Deaths of Chung Hao-Tung and Chiang Bi-Yu

Chung Hao-Tung was one of more than four thousand victims executed in the Nationalist government's White Terror campaign after it fled to Taiwan in 1949. He is mourned here by Chiang Bi-Yu, as performed by Liang Ching. As the scene fades without break into the last scene of the film (previously shown as the film's first scene), which depicts the film crew arriving in China to make the film-within-a-film of *Good Men, Good Women*, Liang Ching's voice-over announces the recent death of the historical Chiang Bi-Yu at the age of seventy-four. The emotional impact of these deaths is sustained by accompanying music that continues throughout the film's showing of the credits, which is retained here.

ACKNOWLEDGMENTS

I am much indebted and deeply thankful to the many people who have aided, abetted, and otherwise inspired my work on this project, among them Julia (Judy) Andrews, Kevin Carr, Dora Ching, Julie Davis, Patricia Failing and Bob Sitton, Feng Bin and Guo Haiwen, film director Lou Ye, Stanley Rosen, Mike and Margaret Wan, and Slavoj Žižek. Eugene Wang, my Harvard sidekick in Chinese cinema studies, Marek Wieczorek, my former colleague in Seattle, and Yingjin Zhang, whose understanding of Chinese film is unsurpassed, offered thorough readings, countless challenging ideas, and thoughtful suggestions, as did my good friend James Morris.

Superb technical assistance with DVD production was given at Princeton's New Media Center by David Hopkins and Lance Herrington, along with Carolyn Guile, who provided both research and wise aesthetic counsel.

At the University of Washington Press, ever the model for author friendliness, director Pat Soden, executive editor Michael Duckworth, and managing editor Marilyn Trueblood all supported this project from start to finish and worked hard to assure the smooth coordination of its many parts. John Stevenson, over Hunanese dim sum, first helped talk me into doing this project and later served as project manager. Mary Ribesky did what a fine text editor is supposed to do, turning many potential slips and awkward falls into real prose. Sigrid Albert provided the original design. The enthusiasm and longtime support of retired editor-in-chief Naomi Pascal and the spirit of the late director Don Ellegood are here too.

This book is dedicated to my wonderful family, Michelle, Emily and David, who have put up with too many books already.

Given the attention in this text to colonialism and regional diversity in Chinese-speaking East Asia, it seems inappropriate to impose a single transliteration system on the various polities represented here. Therefore, while using Pinyin for my own text and translating other writers' Wade-Giles into Pinyin except in the case of published titles, I have retained the transliteration of names, both real and cinematic, just as they appear in cinematic subtitles and film credits. I hope readers will appreciate that whatever confusion results from this is part of what this book is all about. The sole exception I have made is for three characters in the film *Suzhou River*, where neither local standards nor the pronunciation used in the film can be called upon to justify the spellings that appear there in English-language subtitles (Mardar, Moudan, Xia-Ho); I follow the Mandarin standard used elsewhere throughout the film instead (Mada, Mudan, and Xiao Hong). (For a comment on the significance of these names, see chapter 1, note 1.)

I have quoted the English subtitles as given in the films except when there seemed a compelling need to provide my own more accurate translation.

Day by day must men grow farther and farther apart or closer and closer together.

—Shi Nai'an (attributed), *The Water-Margin (Shuihu zhuan)*

. . . the young man or woman writing today has forgotten the problems of the human heart in conflict with itself which alone can make good writing because only that is worth writing about, worth the agony and the sweat. He must learn them again. He must teach himself that the basest of all things is to be afraid; and, teaching himself that, forget it forever, leaving no room in his workshop for anything but the old verities and truths of the heart, the old universal truths lacking which any story is ephemeral and doomed—love and honor and pity and pride and compassion and sacrifice.

—William Faulkner, "Address upon Receiving the Nobel Prize for Literature," December 10, 1950

Introduction

This book began as a bit of self-indulgence. Three Chinese-language films have stood out as my personal favorites in recent years. They were not big box-office hits, but they compelled my attention and admiration in inverse proportion to their popular profile. One of these comes from the People's Republic (Lou Ye's *Suzhou River*, 2000), one from Hong Kong (Yim Ho's *The Day the Sun Turned Cold*, 1994), and one from Taiwan (Hou Hsiao-hsien's *Good Men, Good Women*, 1995). Superficially at least, their stories and styles are as different as their geographic origins, and it did not seem to me at first that they really had all that much in common. Providing a glimpse into the less-than-glamorous world of Shanghai's present-day criminal element, *Suzhou River* takes a page from Alfred Hitchcock in telling the story of a man's pursuit of a woman whose death he imagines he might have caused years earlier when she was a young girl. In *The Day the Sun Turned Cold*, a young man accuses his mother of having murdered his father ten years earlier. The credibility of this charge remains uncertain long into the film, but its mystery is eclipsed by the film's psychodynamic view of social conflict, unusual still among Chinese-language films, and by the film's intriguing parable of the colonial status of Hong Kong. *Good Men, Good Women* is a cinematic puzzler: deeply tragic, spiritually inspired, and one of Taiwan's (indeed, all of Asia's) great film achievements. In it, a movie actress haunted by her own corrupt past dreams of becoming the heroic character she is performing in film. Juxtaposing political and military history with gangland fiction, repeatedly establishing and then dissolving edges and boundaries, its cinematic form mirrors the linguistic, cultural, and political fissures that distinguish Taiwan from China and Taiwan's present from its own past. *Suzhou River* is dynamically edited, with a cinematic speed that reflects the rapid pace of modern Shanghai and packs all the punch that one might anticipate would claim the enthusiasm of a broad American audience. *The Day the Sun Turned Cold* is more traditional in its style and pacing as it plays on—and off of—traditional Chinese cinematic and cultural values. *Good Men, Good Women* slows to a stately pace that actually requires an attention span, more like a deep read than a hip film, as if to signify human values resistant to change despite all the revolutions and generational transitions of the last century.

While all three films have won international awards,[1] none has gained major name recognition thus far in the West. *The Day the Sun Turned Cold* dwells in nearly total obscurity. *Good Men, Good Women* remains one of famed director Hou Hsiao-hsien's least well-received films, even in Taiwan. Only *Suzhou River* currently seems capable of sparking any further international interest. At first, all I was interested in was why these three films in particular seemed so compelling to me, so deserving of critical recognition, and why they seemed not to stand alone but to occupy the same aesthetic and cultural ground. What inner vision did they share?

Gradually, the more I indulged in speculation about these films, the less indulgent my efforts seemed to be. The films are all remarkable for their intellectual depth and range, their layered complexity, their emotional sobriety, their appeal to a sophisticated film audience rather than a mass market, their determined critique of contemporary culture, their integrated use of both Chinese and Western cinematic traditions to achieve this, and the resonance of their moral voice. Not only do they seem to "prove themselves" in terms of film artistry—a match for the very best films that have come out of that part of the world in recent decades—but they also share a set of underlying thematic concerns and stylistic means. They display a wariness about China's social disposition toward psychological conformity and enforced consensus. They challenge any singular definition of what constitutes a "Chinese" cultural identity in these times of rapid diversification and decentralization, rejecting any pretensions toward a national "unity" which would sweep Taiwan and Hong Kong into the all-embracing fold of a central Chinese population and Beijing authority, or which—internal to the People's Republic—would pave over the local distinctiveness of sites like Shanghai and deny them individual and alternate paths to the future. Common to their approach in deconstructing the narrative of a unitary Chinese mythos is their deployment of dual personalities (with actresses playing multiple roles in two of the films and an uncertain maternal "identity" in the third), their use of nonlinear temporal sequences, the reliance of their narration on emotionally conflicted and objectively indeterminate memory, an unusual affinity for ambiguity and unresolvable situations, a preoccupation with deception and betrayal, a fascination with criminal behavior and the underworld as both a mirror of and an alternative to traditional power structures, a probing engagement with the uncertain morality of social justice, the unfolding of complex Oedipal relationships, an exploration of the traditional avoidance of public shame and the suppressed expression of private guilt, a Chinese manifestation of the principles of *cinema verite*, and a knowledgeable application of *film noir* style.

These films are not "typical" Chinese-language films, but they are by no means alone. They exemplify the ever-deepening integration of East-West cinematic and intellectual culture. In viewing them, there is nothing of the primitive (or supposedly primitive or pseudo-primitive) that is an essential ingredient for an "exoticizing" or "Orientalizing" reception. These are highly sophisticated films and do not strike one (not even the theoretically inclined) as the obvious product of an "other" culture any more than do the films of Jean-Luc Godard or Ingmar Bergman or Yasujiro Ozu. Shanghai, Hong Kong, and Taipei are their places of production (as well as their geopolitical problems), and these places are no less sophisticated today and not much more physically remote from New York or Hollywood than are Paris or Stockholm or Tokyo. Rather, these films are markers of urban cultures, for better or worse, they impress an American audience as comfortably familiar (or familiarly uncomfortable) and as works of art made in the global here-and-now, even as they sometimes depict the there-and-then. In discussion of them, my references and comparisons are thus as frequently to Americana and to European sources as they are to Orientalia. It is not always the *actuality* (that is to say, some explicit reference by the film artists) that calls forth particular comparisons as much as it is the *aptness*. These film directors are knowledgeable in both Chinese and Western film culture (Yim Ho studied in London; Lou Ye specifically studied the film-school styles of New York University and UCLA at the Beijing Film Academy), and they are just as familiar with Alfred Hitchcock, John Cassavetes, and Michelangelo Antonioni, not to mention Japan's Ozu, as they are with China's Cai Chusheng, Yuan Muzhi, and Xie Jin. They also know the Western past, not just the Chinese present: they have an ear for Schubert, just as they do for Cui Jian; they may be as well read in Dostoevsky and Faulkner as they are in Lu Xun, Shen Congwen, Su Tong, and Wang Shuo; they know both classical Freud and his Lacanian and post-Lacanian by-products.

There is, of course, nothing new about Western sourcing in Chinese cinema. Ideological assertions that the medium is essentially "alien" to China—mechanistic and inherently exploitative[2]—ignore and run contrary to the central role of mechanicity and modularity in China's thirty-five-hundred-year history of artistic production[3] as well as to the speed and ease with which China embraced and adopted the medium, dating all the way back to 1896.[4] Chinese-language films from Yuan Muzhi's *Street Angel* (1937) to Wang Xiaoshuai's *Beijing Bicycle* (2001) have been influenced by particular American and European sources, yet they have transformed them almost beyond recognition,[5] just as their literary counterparts have done (Mo Yan, author of *Red Sorghum*, 1987, cites Faulkner's 1929 *The Sound and the Fury* as one of "two particular works [that] have had the greatest impact on me"[6]). Not only have well-known films like Chen Kaige's *Farewell My Concubine* (1993) utilized some of Hollywood's most sophisticated techniques, John Woo's films, beginning with *A Better Tomorrow*

(1986), have had their own reverse impact.[7] It has even been argued that "film in China has *always* been of a transnational character."[8] What is thus new in the way these three films help define a new stage in the development of Chinese cinema is not mere borrowing. Their influence lies not so much in their technical means—although there is some of that, too—as in their devising of cinematic means to penetrate the film's own surface and realize an emphasis unusual in Chinese film on inner, psychological "reality" and psychopathology.

With few exceptions, Chinese film, like traditional Chinese literature and theater, has fronted typologies rather than complex, conflicted, credibly individualized personalities. The traditional Chinese narrative pattern presents a stable character confronted with a fated situation, just as Western melodrama tends to do.[9] This trio of films, by contrast, presents characters whose surface appearances and public behaviors both disguise and ultimately reveal complex inner lives of unresolved psychic forces. In addition to the other features mentioned above, these three films are united by their exploration of lives that revolve around guilt and loneliness, isolation and desire, the pain of parental rejection and generational alienation, narcissism and escapism, emotional repression and compensatory behavior—in all, a dimension not yet common in Chinese-language film.[10] In the People's Republic, it has long been a rationale of socialist critics that the traditional "hollowness" of characters' inner beings, not by neglect but by conscious design, constitutes a kind of "respect" for the mass audience, empowering each member of the audience to fill in these personalities. In contrast, the comparative psychological "concreteness" of characters in "art films" beginning in the mid-1980s was subjected to considerable official criticism as foreclosing the audience's "pleasure of being cofilmmakers."[11] But it might equally well be argued that this theatrical mode, essentially melodramatic in form, has in reality helped to mold a more unified audience while denying the Chinese audience diverse models by which to acknowledge and explore the complexities and diversity of their own individual motivations and the internal mechanisms of conflict resolution, while the "art films" have opened up a new dimension in the public arena.

If the development of this psychological dimension represents the movement of Chinese culture closer to that of the West—with film as a cultural force that effects collective perceptions and changes the public psyche—the function of all this as a cinematic mechanism in the films discussed here bears directly on questions of specific local concern and to the overarching questions of "What is China?" and "What is China *today?*" These films are all concerned with issues of local identity, social justice, and social maturation in a post-colonized or still-colonized world. The framework of *Suzhou River* is the still-living memory of Shanghai, the "whore of the East," colonized by Britain, France, and the United States, which subsequently—as a result of this colonial "cultural pollution"—was treated as a pariah (in effect, ideologically recolonized) by Mao's regime.[12] De-colonized only in the last decade, Shanghai has assumed economic leadership of a nation still in the midst of an identity crisis as it cashes in its "revolutionary romanticism" for a more pragmatic brand of material-ism.[13] As the third-generation Communist Party leaders, many of them Shanghai bred and led, seem in the increasingly cynical public imagination to be fattening themselves and their families by means of their political connections, Mao Zedong's stern dictum that "a revolution is not a dinner party" has been replaced by the popular slogan "a revolution *is* a dinner party."[14] *Suzhou River* ponders a future framed by the loss of the older values: community spirit, ideological fidelity, and urban romance. The symbolic structure of *The Day the Sun Turned Cold* derives from Hong Kong's reversion from British to (Communist) Chinese domination; betrayal and the high price of honesty are its concerns. For *Good Men, Good Women*, the framework is the island of Taiwan, fought over and colonized by a succession of Manchus, Japanese, Nationalist Chinese, and (however indirectly) Americans; like *The Godfather*, it probes the very nature of corruption and its roots in systems of belief and unquestioned faith. What lies at the core of its concerns is the preservation of honor and compassion within the fighting family of man.

The interaction of Chinese and Western film has become one of the central areas of interest for Western scholars of Chinese culture and cinema culture. Academic initiatives in regard to this issue range between the now-popular position (sensitive to the pitfalls of globalization as an extension of Western imperialism) that Western influence in both filmmaking ("Hollywood hegemony") and film criticism ("Western interpretive authority") corrupts and effectively "recolonizes" Chinese film and culture, and the contrary position (which I share) that the former belief, by implicitly prescribing a cultural quarantine, primitivizes (re-Orientalizes) Chinese cinematic culture and denies it a legitimate, interactive, and beneficial place in world culture.[15] What is important, it seems to me, is not whether Chinese film ought to engage with Western cinematic culture—that is inevitable and always has been—but how it does so. There are, of course, many dimensions to this, including the Chinese filmmakers' response to Western reception and, particularly, to international film festivals. But even among those films made by Chinese filmmakers in the West, one can see enormous variation, from John Woo's recent film *Windtalkers* (2002), which proves capable of reproducing (even while updating) every John Ford cliché about the American "primitive"/noble savage while simultaneously revisiting all the shallowest clichés of 1950s Hollywood war films, to Ang Lee's *The Ice Storm* (1997) (adapting Rick Moody's novel[16]), which by contrast provides chilling insight into the betrayal of American family values in the 1970s and outstrips most of its American counterparts in doing so.[17] Although *all* such films are worthy of study, whether deemed original or highly derivative, the three films looked at in this volume strike me as representing the most benign products of the transnational cinema phenomenon, representing the enrichment of Chinese culture through an engagement *on their own terms* with non-Chinese cultures, challenging all they interact with, recombining what they borrow with material from China's own mature native culture, and achieving an original result.

The most significant Western component, then, of each of these films—the internal psychology, the construction and contemplation of neurosis as a vehicle for studying the functions and dysfunction of culture and politics among the "members" of the Chinese-speaking "family"—operates not as an uninvited global intrusion, forcibly colonizing or commodifying the Chinese subject for delivery to a foreign audience. To the contrary, at the same time as they represent an ongoing, outward expansion of Chinese-speaking artists and intellectuals into the arena of global culture, these films primarily address internal concerns. Their engagement with Western cinematic, literary, and psychological models, with Hitchcock and *film noir*, with Freud and Oedipal dynamics, with Dostoevsky's double-characters and his inner monologue, with the fractured time sequences and shifting, sometimes unlocatable narrative voices introduced and best represented by Faulkner, is a cinematic appropriation applied to their own chosen ends. But if putting a "Chinese face" on Hitchcock, or on Freud or Faulkner, like Deng Xiaoping's famous "socialism with a Chinese face" or "socialism with Chinese characteristics," is much less than submission to a foreign influence, it is also much more than *mere* appropriation. It is a carefully considered attachment of one's own "face"—one's prestige, one's integrity—to that of another, defining a voluntary, sophisticated, and artistically permeable interface of two cultural systems: global engagement, not Oriental submission.

Chinese history offers well-remembered instances of cultural infusion in which borrowings eventually became so sinicized as to virtually breed a new species. Buddhism provides the classic example,[18] but while that degree of sinicization does not exist here—not yet, anyhow—the process of appropriation and globalization is scarcely new to China. Still, all three films discussed here take part in a theory-driven, post-colonial, post-socialist film tradition to which mainland China, Hong Kong, and Taiwan have all begun to add their own significant contributions, giving rise to a cinema of regional deconstruction and moral reconstruction.[19] Indeed, each of these three films challenges the hegemonic process itself, and they unite in mutual rejection of the manipulative, authoritarian qualities cynically exploited as a means of "preserving" an otherwise historically ambiguous Chinese nation. Yet post-colonialism is not all so clear-cut, and elements of local self-definition often combine readily with long-standing desires and newfound freedoms to cross political boundaries and bridge cultural divides. So it is superficially ironic at most that these three films from three different regional cultures, proclaiming local diversity and representing three local variants of East Asia's Chinese-speaking cultures, should nonetheless correspond so closely in their moral principles, their cinematic means, and the international sources to which they turn for intellectual support. At a deeper level this similarity ought not to surprise, for embedded in the increasing globalization represented by these films is an ontology that involves economic and intellectual cooperation between the PRC, Hong Kong, and Taiwan as much as it does with the audiences and ideas of America, Europe, and Japan.[20] Rather than imagining "global" and "local" as dialectical antagonists and being perplexed by the current, simultaneous rise of both, we would do better (at least) to triangulate this pair with nationalism, at whose expense global means operate to facilitate local strategies in the increasingly decentralized Chinese-speaking world today.

All of this shrinking and then bursting of boundaries becomes evident in the production of these films. Hou Hsiao-hsien's Taiwan-based film was partly filmed in Guangdong, and its compelling musical theme was Taiwan-composed to a hybrid Taiwan-Celtic inspiration, a global concoction blending Western church organ, Irish harp, Chinese lute, Chinese wood flute, and muffled snare drum.[21] Yim Ho's Hong Kong–based film was shot in the People's Republic with a largely mainland cast and set to Japanese-composed, Schubert-inspired chamber music. Lou Ye's *Suzhou River*, post-produced in Germany, features the independent-minded music of Taiwanese-aboriginal pop star A-Mei (Chang Hui Mei), whose singing of the Taiwan national anthem at the inauguration of independence-minded Taiwan President Chen Shuibian in May 2000 led to a ban on her concertizing in the People's Republic.[22] Among other border-crossing endeavors by these same filmmakers, Hong Kong's Yim Ho shuttles back and forth between the fanatical political primitivism of the PRC during the Cultural Revolution and Taiwan's equally frenetic emergence into cyber-modernity in *King of Chess* (1989, co-directed with Tsui Hark), while Taiwan's Hou Hsiao-hsien both co-produced *King of Chess* and served as executive producer for PRC filmmaker Zhang Yimou's Academy Award–nominated *Raise the Red Lantern* (1991).

It is also characteristic of the current generation of Chinese artists that they fully intend for their art to remain open to a range of interpretations, permitting even their own understanding of their work to change and develop over time.[23] Such an intent may be taken for granted in the West, but the official aesthetic doctrine of the People's Republic still remains that which Chairman Mao proclaimed in 1942: "Our writings [and our art] should help [the people] to unite, to make progress, to press ahead with *one* heart and *one* mind, to discard what is backward and develop what is revolutionary, and should certainly not do the opposite."[24] Official doctrine rejects ambiguity; but allegory, which literally says one thing while meaning another, is China's age-old language of communication, while China's rhetorical analogic has always left ample room for various interpretations.[25] How many different levels of meaning these films were intended to invoke is anyone's guess. I certainly don't imagine that the interpretations I present here are unassailable, exhaustive, theoretically "correct," or in any way "the last word" on these three films or on the larger body of works that they represent. I happily acknowledge the subjectivity of my views.

If the social content of these films were all that drew our attention to them, it might be sufficient just to fill out in brief the outlines already set forth here. The academic tradition of systematically turning art into social criticism is still relatively new and owes greatly to the American intellectual historian Vernon Louis Parrington. In 1927, at the outset of his seminal Pulitzer Prize–winning classic, *Main Currents in*

American Thought: An Interpretation of American Literature from the Beginnings to 1920, Parrington wrote, "I have chosen to follow the broad path of our political, economic, and social development, rather than the narrower belletristic."[26] Parrington was the first, for example, to treat Huck Finn as a commentary on social mores and historical reconstruction in the post–Civil War age of the late nineteenth century; today his accomplishments are taken for granted throughout much of the world, and it typifies much of the current writing on a subject as far afield from his own as Chinese cinema. Social critique is a critical element of these films, more indirect than direct by way of stylistic routing, but self-conscious and deeply felt. Given that the critique is often directed at the politicization itself of daily life, a political interpretation of these films may seem ironic. But these films are nothing if not ironical and densely layered with competing claims for our attention. In addition to their offerings of social commentary, these films are structured as visual art, and the visible artistry with which they meet us and by which their commentary is delivered—generically, inadequately attended to thus far in Chinese cinematic studies—remains my deepest concern in all that follows.[27]

For an art historian, the sociopolitical and the "belletristic" are mutually interactive and heuristically indiscrete. Narrativity and imagery are not oppositional and not necessarily even alternatives, but are often one and the same thing. This is true in all cases where film achieves its capacity as a visual art. And it is particularly true with mainland Chinese cinema, where the censorship of film scripts in their textual formulation shifts the filmmakers' primary negotiable space to the realm of unspoken images, a richly encoded visual realm where textual pursuit alone may falter but where the art historian travels most comfortably. Taiwan director Ang Lee has written in reference to his film *The Ice Storm* that "the power of the novel is to make of this moment no more and no less than what it is. It is an image that has the force of memory, and for that reason an image that has more meaning than any theme or story or even emotion can give it."[28] The emphatic visuality of so many Chinese-language films accounts for one of the chief features of this publication: unlike almost all publications on Chinese-language cinema, which feature publicity stills for their illustrations—sharp, often even slick, but painfully inauthentic—and therefore deprive readers of a legitimate viewing experience, this volume exclusively illustrates downloaded film frames, which, despite some loss in clarity, nonetheless represent images that actually occur in the films discussed. As I protested in an earlier publication, "Virtually every illustration published in Chinese film studies could be analyzed for the misinformation provided. . . . One can scarcely conceive of an analogous situation in literary studies (writing about Shakespeare, perhaps, while quoting only Holinshed or Marlowe) or imagine its being tolerated academically."[29] At the very least, I hope that this short work contributes toward an increased attentiveness to the visual artistry of Chinese-language film and gives the highest priority to the works themselves rather than to preconceptions brought their way.

CHAPTER 1

Hitchcock with a Chinese Face: *Suzhou River*

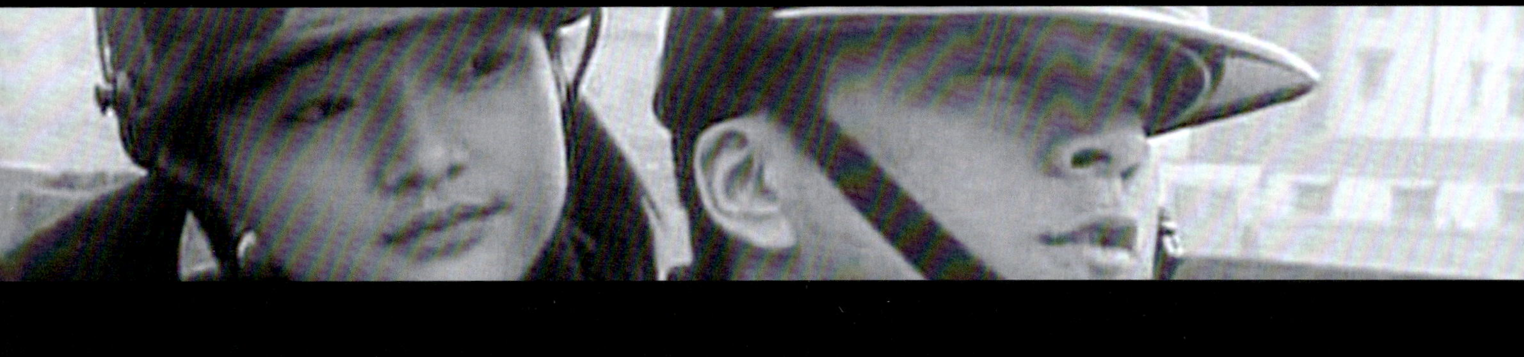

In today's popular culture, there are two phenomena which exert an ever-lasting power of fascination on so-called "postmodern" theory: Alfred Hitchcock and film noir.

—Slavoj Žižek, *Enjoy Your Symptom!*

Suzhou River (Suzhou he). Director: Lou Ye; Cinematography: Wang Yu; Film editing: Karl Riedl; Music: Jorg Lemberg; Art direction: Li Zhuoyi; Cast: Zhou Xun (Mudan [Moudan or Peony] and Meimei), Jia Hongsheng (Mada [Mardar]), Nai An (Xiao Hong [Xia-Ho or Little Red]), Hua Zhongkai (Lao B.), Yao Anlian (Boss); Screenplay: Lou Ye; Production: Nai An, Philippe Bober; Studio: Lou Ye Dream Factory and Essential Film Produktion GMBH; 2000; 83 minutes

Suzhou River

PLOT SUMMARY

The film begins in total darkness with a woman's voice (Meimei's, but she is not yet identified), which serves as a prologue and sets the theme: "If I left you someday, would you pursue me? . . . Would you pursue me forever?"

(Shift in characters . . .) Mudan is the adolescent daughter of a wealthy, divorced bootlegger whose free time is spent with prostitutes. Whenever one of his "girlfriends" arrives, Mudan is shuffled off to her aunt's by the motorcycle courier Mada. Gradually the two become intimate, with Mada reluctant but providing a substitute for the mother- less child's loss of her remaining parent's love. But Mada is a man of Shanghai's corrupt back alleys and is soon drawn into a kidnap plot by his sometime girlfriend, Xiao Hong.[1] While Mudan is held as hostage, her betrayal by Mada is matched with Xiao Hong's betrayal and murder by Lao B., the third party to this criminal misadventure. Discovering how little has been asked for by Mada and paid by her father for her freedom ("Forty- five thousand?" she cries. "I'm that cheap!?"), Mudan escapes and in front of the disbe- lieving Mada she jumps into Suzhou River, vowing to "turn into a mermaid and come looking for you."

Years later, Mada returns from prison still hoping to find Mudan, whose body was never found. Revisiting the bar where he plotted the kidnapping, Mada discovers Mudan's look-alike, Meimei—grown up and performing as a mermaid in an underwater floor show. Meimei denies any knowledge of Mada or Mudan. Is she amnesiac? Insincere? Her increasing attraction to Mada and sympathy for his quest arouses the ire of Meimei's unnamed videographer boyfriend, who has purportedly taped and has narrated much of this film from the outset and who belatedly enters the narrative at this point as an engaged participant, arranging for Mada to be beaten up by the bartender's bouncers. Mada

Although he worked in the so-called "B" genres of mystery, suspense, and horror, Alfred Hitchcock has gradually become one of the most celebrated film directors of all time and probably the most widely studied by American film scholars. First and foremost an entertainer by his own accounting, Hitchcock has become far more influential after his death than one might ever have anticipated during his lifetime.[2] His most successful films, such as *Vertigo*, *Rear Window*, and *Psycho*, have inspired spin-offs by countless directors, from Brian de Palma to Mel Brooks to Hitchcock himself.[3] Add to this list for the first time a Chinese film—*Suzhou River*, written and directed by Lou Ye.

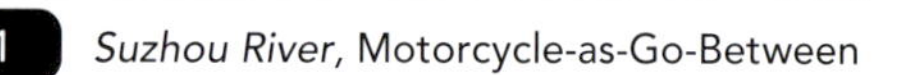

1   *Suzhou River*, Motorcycle-as-Go-Between   **2**   *Suzhou River*, "I'm That Cheap!?"

As a successor to China's so-called "Fifth Generation" of filmmakers, Lou Ye is among the first Chinese directors to study Western film from the outset of their career. By the time of Lou Ye's birth, in 1965, the last of Hitchcock's most important films were already done, and by the time of Lou Ye's graduation from the Beijing Film Academy,[4] the late Alfred Hitchcock had become an international legend. Set in the narrow lanes and alleys of old Shanghai, Lou Ye's third film,[5] *Suzhou River*, borrows from Alfred Hitchcock the idea of a woman betrayed by her own male protector and a lost love whose apparent death the protector-betrayer cannot accept (figs. 1 and 2). His fantasies about her possible survival lead to another woman, whose striking similarity to the

3   *Suzhou River*, Mudan and Prostitute

4   *Suzhou River*, Blonde Meimei

woman lost leaves him and the audience unsure whether he is deluded or not. The confusion between the presumed victim and her living double (both roles performed with great versatility by Zhou Xun[6]) makes a mystery of romance itself, darkly questioning the nature of romantic pursuit (figs. 3 and 4). The resemblance between Lou Ye's and Hitchcock's *noir* films, especially between *Suzhou River* and Hitchcock's *Vertigo*, was intended and well noted by most critics, though perhaps not evident to a casual audience. How many viewers, whether Chinese or American, will recognize that in both *Vertigo* and *Suzhou River* the "reincarnated" heroine sits at her dressing table lit by green and pink from the neon sign just outside her window (figs. 5 and 6),

5   *Vertigo*, Judy's Room

6   *Suzhou River*, Meimei's Dressing Room

accompanied by a similar undercurrent of melancholic, Bernard Herrmann–inspired string music?

In Chinese artistic practice, such resemblance is a throwback to what traditional critics described with the term *fang*, translatable as a "transformative imitation" and signifying a referential homage[7] (figs. 7 and 8). A poet, painter, or calligrapher works in the style of another, but always with a twist. The idea is not to copy with the kind of slavish traditionalism often ascribed to latter-day Confucian culture but rather to develop *creatively* on borrowed material, as Beethoven did with Bach, Mozart, and the little-known Anton Diabelli, or as an academic essay does with references and

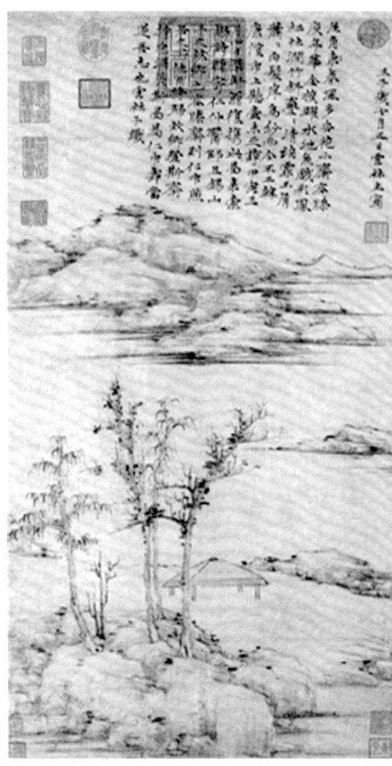

7 Ni Zan, *The Rongxi Studio*, 1372. National Palace Museum, Taiwan (from Wen Fong, *Possessing the Past*)

8 Shitao, *Landscape After Ni Zan*, ca.1700. Princeton University Art Museum

9 *The Lady Vanishes*

quotations from other scholars, often leading in directions quite different, unimagined, or even contrary to the original work. Unconcerned with intellectual tradition, one local film reviewer labeled *Suzhou River* a "shameless rip-off," ignoring in its attention to borrowed trivia the emphatic contrast between Hitchcock's determined cynicism and Lou Ye's inspired contestation of contemporary Chinese alienation.[8] At any rate, in thinking of one film when we see the other, we are bound to ask: what happens when East meets West, when Hitchcock comes to China, or rather, when China comes to Hitchcock?

The "disappearance that everybody denies"[9] is a theme that in one form or another runs through numerous Hitchcock films, from his early works in England like *The Lady Vanishes* (fig. 9) and *Foreign Correspondent* through later Hollywood products like *Rear Window* and *Psycho*. With this disappearance, which everybody denies— except, of course, the hero—one's identity may suddenly be up for grabs, along with one's sanity. The reality or utter unreality of perceptions is put into question, and the audience is in for a bumpy ride trying to decide just who is crazy and who is not. Through this theme, Hitchcock abuses his hero, manipulating him into the position of having either to reject his own perceptions as hallucinatory or else resist a conspiracy of strangers by clinging so obsessively to his own viewpoint that he is publicly branded as crazy anyhow. It is a unite-and-divide mechanism by which the support or rejection of the hero's viewpoint distinguishes the sympathetic from unsympathetic characters and typically leads romantically to some form of hero-heroine bonding. While the audience is bound to sympathize with the hero, they are left to guess which of the other characters will lean in what directions and who, melodramatically, will eventually lend the vital support needed to bring the truth to light. Hitchcock's films provide a variety of masterful twists and turns on this device, artfully "ripping himself off" (or *fang*ing himself, as it were). In *Dial M for Murder,* having failed in the hired murder of his wife, a husband seeks to have her branded with the criminality of her would-be killer and executed for slaying her own assailant. In *North by Northwest,* the hero is made to watch himself vanish as various Cold War factions fight to appropriate his identity. In *Psycho,* it is the insane villain who tests the sanity of others, denying his mother's disappearance and destroying those who threaten her continuing authority over him.

The distinctive feature of *Vertigo,* which *Suzhou River* most conspicuously resembles, is that the lady vanishes not once but twice. *Vertigo*'s neurotic male lead, alone among the film's characters, gradually comes to doubt and then to deny her disappearance. Along the way, the hero's manipulative obsession with the heroine's *imagined* death leads to a destructive repetition of events by which he ends up *actually* destroying her through his own actions. In other words, although his motives are different, through his psychological defects he callously replicates the behavior of the villain who originally plotted the victimization of both heroine and hero. As in many Hitchcock films, pathology finds a way to overcome all obstacles. *Vertigo*'s acting may

10   *Psycho*, Mother

be stiff and problematic, but the twisted plot makes for an endlessly engaging intellectual puzzle.[10]

In *Vertigo*, as in *Suzhou River*, the male lead (Scottie, Mada) both becomes intimate with and betrays the woman he has been hired to protect (Madeleine, Mudan). In both films, the lady vanishes but seems to return from the dead (as Judy, as Meimei)—at least in the eyes of the failed hero. He imagines himself guilty of her death yet obsesses over finding her still alive, while others understandably regard him as demented. And before either film is over, she has vanished again and he has become—for real, this time—the agent of her demise. But in Lou Ye's film, nothing goes without a further twist on Hitchcock's twisted original. James Stewart's Scottie is a good cop who fails to realize he's going bad, driven downward not by criminal intent but by his own neurotic flaws. Stewart's counterpart in *Suzhou River*, the lowly motorcycle courier Mada, is morally adrift in Shanghai's criminal underground when he kidnaps his own young charge for ransom, but subsequently, after risking his life in a last-minute attempt to save her, and then after serving a prison sentence, he is driven by guilt and romantic inspiration to pursue reform, redress, and redemption. In the wake of his pursuit—of the wrong party, as it turns out—things go horribly wrong, much as in *Vertigo*, but in the end Mada's quest for redemption inspires the mistaken female's spiritual awakening. Successively, the young and exuberant Mudan, the subdued but persistent Mada, and the proud and self-directed Meimei manage to inspire each other, and in conclusion, they challenge the audience to follow a trajectory quite the opposite of *Vertigo*'s Scottie.[11]

Every Hitchcock fan knows what that director means by the term "MacGuffin." A MacGuffin is a gimmick, a cinematic red herring that drives the plot (but not straightforwardly). The device has little intrinsic meaning of its own and is quickly jettisoned once it has served its purpose.[12] The best-known example, perhaps, is the embezzlement that Janet Leigh pulls off in the early minutes of *Psycho:* a clever distraction intended to drive her into confines of the Bates Motel before the audience realizes what is happening. Even then, we're left for a few minutes more to imagine that Norman Bates is merely some offbeat Peeping Tom, until with unheralded and unforgettable suddenness the stunned audience is introduced to the film's central plot of a boy and his disappearing mother (fig. 10). In this regard, *Suzhou River* both borrows from and one-up's Hitchcock's *Vertigo*. In *Vertigo*, the first disappearance of the heroine is the MacGuffin; what we're really interested in is how the hero deals with her after she returns "from the dead" and what it reveals about his own neuroses. In *Suzhou River*, virtually the entire film is turned into a MacGuffin. We're long interested in the hero's pursuit of the reincarnated heroine before we discover in the last moments of the film that the moral of this tale is best embodied neither by the vanished girl, Mudan, nor by the reincarnation she's supposed to be, but instead by someone she evidently was not but *now* becomes. Meimei, as spectator, is so transformed by the events we have all been watching that she confirms the lasting meaning of the film: fidelity matters more than identity, and in the end optimism rises to challenge the pervasive cynicism of contemporary Shanghai. If, as it turns out, Meimei wasn't actually the reincarnated Mudan, now at last she turns out to be her spiritual heir. Until the very end, Meimei is as much as anyone down in the theater seats a mere spectator to Mada's obsession. But in the end, it is through her that the audience is interrogated: will we follow her response or not? Ironically, then, the real MacGuffin in *Suzhou River* is the Hitchcockian reference itself. The master director and *noir* cynic is an apt embodiment of contemporary China's own ability, through unimaginable twists and turns, to reshape and redirect its energies in unpredicted directions—each of them fascinating but all of them colored by the view that the human psyche is perverse and that romance is doomed to failure. The distinctive turn in *Suzhou River*'s meandering course is a channel away from that dark cynicism. The Hitchcock face and the "Chinese face" are not all that different; what is different here is *Suzhou River*'s subversion of China's, and simultaneously of Hitchcock's own, dark values. *Suzhou River* turns Hitchcock on his head, or at least on his side, offering an alternative based on fidelity and romance. Actress Zhou Xun's youthful exuberance as Mudan (*Suzhou River* DVD, Scene 2) and proud self-determination as Meimei (*Suzhou River* DVD, Scene 3) are a perfect foil for the moody understatement and psychological isolation of Jia Hongsheng in the role of Mada, conflicted about his purpose, as is China itself.[13] Born of the first generation, with no experience of the Maoist state's claims on the individual and its legacy of betrayal, the impulsive Mudan presents a challenge to the older Mada and Meimei that is nothing short of counterrevolutionary. "Romance evokes real emotion," Lou Ye has said. "In real life, there's little romance of any real quality—you need to evoke it, just like when you're watching or making a film."[14] "People need this kind of romanticism in order to face the harshness of life."[15]

Vertigo's primary tensions all stem from classical Freudian theory. After all, Hitchcock was increasingly involved with psychoanalysis during its great American heyday in the 1950s and brought it to the fore in many ways.[16] Mental disturbance frequently lay at the root of the criminal activity he explored. In films like *Spellbound* and *Marnie,* he approached mental problems much as he did his cinematic crimes: as in figuring out who dunnit, one had only to discover the cause of a mental disturbance for the neurosis to be resolved. A good catharsis was very much like a good mystery solved, and vice versa. The cinematic Hitchcock didn't worry much about the uncertain outcome of actual therapeutic practice,[17] yet at the same time most of his films exhibited a pessimistic preoccupation with the human propensity toward neurosis and psychosis, toward obsession, perversion, and criminality.

Suzhou River, in its pattern of betrayal, loss, and pursuit of recovery, is less concerned with the intricacies of crime-solving or developmental psychology than it is with overcoming a collective neurosis, with encountering and transcending a corrupting cynicism that originates not with the individual but arises in the social sphere and operates in the personal psyche by extension. Like many of China's greatest modern narratives, from Cao Xueqin's eighteenth-century *Dream of the Red Chamber* to Ba Jin's early twentieth-century *Family, Suzhou River* is concerned with the social obstacles to human freedom and romantic self-expression, with fate (*ming*) and coping with fate (fig. 11). It is, indeed, a cry for a society that in recent times has swung broadly from collective political frenzy to impersonal economic fervor to become more romantic, more idealistic, more personal, for people to become more concerned (even obsessed) with each other rather than remain trapped by materialist ideologies. Like the romantic novels *Dream of the Red Chamber* and *Family*, it is not as much focused on plot (though the plot is compelling) as it is on rising beyond narrative detail to a higher plane and purpose.

The psychological thrust of Hitchcock's films, more often than not, is classically Oedipal, turning upon the unresolved sexual attachment of the hero to a dominant mother, which blocks his capacity to attach appropriately to a romantic, espousable female.[18] *Psycho*'s Norman Bates is the extreme case of this, but Jeffries in *Rear Window* (fig. 35), Thornhill in *North by Northwest* (fig. 12), Mitch in *Marnie,* and Scottie in *Vertigo*, among others, all share this affliction. The Oedipal attachment to mom is not only a fetish in Freudian theory but also something of an artistic obsession with

     HITCHCOCK WITH A CHINESE FACE

11 *Family*, Like a Tomb

12 *North by Northwest*, Mother

Hitchcock—a fetish about a fetish. The shift in most professional psychology circles in more recent decades from emphasis on the tension between childhood sexual fantasy and repressed trauma to cognitive, behavioral, cultural, and biochemical explanations of personality development and psychopathology need not bother us here: the psychological "reality" discussed here is not conceived of as clinically valid (or invalid) but as a cultural phenomenon which, in the words of Jean-Luc Godard, "is neither art nor life but something in between,"[19] one with a life of its own in cinema and the public imagination. Irving Schneider has written that "If psychiatry had not existed, the movies would have to invent it . . . [for] both movies and psychiatry have as their prime focus human thought, emotions, behavior, and, above all, human motivation." But in order to appreciate the dynamics of international cinema, one also needs to account for the varied psychological norms of emotion and motivation which have flourished in divergent cultures, past and present.[20] Efforts to construct a Chinese developmental model that might provide a culture-specific equivalent to Freudian psychodynamic principles have failed on the same grounds that Freudian theory itself falls short of universal relevance: "for treating traditional China as an undifferentiated cultural entity; for largely ignoring problems of regional, class, and individual variation in Chinese society . . . ; and for the fairly unchanging and stereotypical picture of Chinese 'modal character' which results."[21] Nonetheless, even in the absence of psychodynamic models, certain relational tendencies of traditional family behavior can be fairly reliably observed within an anthropological schema,[22] and for the typical Chinese family a different mechanism is needed to understand emotional and social dysfunction, one that is virtually the opposite of Oedipal blockage. As Eugene Wang has noted in commenting on *Red Sorghum*, "As the aspired-to stillness and passivity [in Chinese social culture] have touches of femininity, femininity itself becomes a condition highly aspired to. Instead of being afflicted by castration anxiety, the problematic of the lack is quite reversed in the Chinese cultural context. It is the man who lacks."[23]

In traditional Chinese society, lifelong submission to a dominant parent is healthy; maladjustment emerges from a parental attachment *so weak* that self-determination threatens the parental right to dictate espousement; dysfunction emerges from romantic affection *so strong* that it supersedes the filial responsibility *(xiao)* to one's parents or in-laws. Self-directed romantic attachments like that of the third-century B.C.E. poet Sima Xiangru to his wife Zhuo Wenjun were occasionally celebrated but only as exceptions. More typically, internal conflict between competing desires, between romance and filiality, can lead to an impasse in which sex must become sublimated into political or religious activity, or can lead to a rupture with one's parents and family, or both. In the two semi-autobiographical Chinese novels already mentioned, *Dream of the Red Chamber* and *Family*, such maladjustments lead predictably to the death of the romantic heroine and an interruption of the hero's narrative passage.[24] In *Dream of the Red Chamber*, the hero eventually renounces family and world for a sublimated orbit in the company of Daoist immortals; in Ba Jin's *Family*, resentment toward family authority and "feudal" stagnation ultimately lead the hero onto the path of political anarchism.

In urban Chinese society today, marriage by choice rather than by parental arrangement is now the norm, but in psychological terms the transition to "modernity" is still incomplete. In theory, women may "hold up half of the sky" and marriage may be a "partnership," but in reality marriage remains afflicted by centuries of patriarchal tradition: males frequently remain emotionally remote from their wives ("the interaction between husband and wife is not overly charged with either positive or negative emotions [and] is indeed a secondary relationship in the context of the family"[25]), understanding love as sex, with the result that 30 percent of women reportedly suffer *significant* spousal abuse and more than a quarter of the entire world's suicides are by Chinese women.[26] And so, like a typical Hitchcockian neurotic male, but hardly unusual and not particularly "unhealthy" by Chinese standards, *Suzhou River*'s Mada seems all but incapable of romantic attachment. Despite his evident attractiveness to young women, throughout the first part of the film he regularly stays up all night alone, voyeuristically watching videotapes, and no sooner does a romantic attachment to Mudan erupt than he agrees to kidnap her for ransom. Beyond this, it remains an open question in the latter part of the film whether he (like Scottie) can pursue anyone less threatening than the idealized conception of a vanished female. In both films, the hero's conflicted effort to attach to an ideal female character leads to disaster for hero and heroine alike. There is a push-pull attitude of hero toward heroine, attraction matched (or outweighed) by resistance. Hitchcock captures this tension with the metaphor of vertigo, a condition in which the overt fear of falling ("falling" in love representing castration anxiety in Freudian terms) is heightened by the repressed desire to jump (figs. 45 and 17). The result is Hamlet-like paralysis, or impotence.[27]

The audience is treated to a dramatic spell of dizziness in the opening scenes of both *Vertigo* and *Suzhou River* (figs. 13 and 14; *Suzhou River* DVD, Scene 1) In the

13   *Vertigo*, Vertigo

14   *Suzhou River*, Seasick

latter film, the audience is introduced to the aquatic tale by such an unsettling sensation of seasickness that Dramamine ought to be handed out with the popcorn. No sooner does the narrative begin than the image begins to pitch and roll wildly as the camera navigates Shanghai's notorious Suzhou "river" (or creek, or sewer). The visual impulse toward actual nausea is intensified by the film's grainy texture, derived from the film's conceit that it was actually photographed by the narrator's hand-held digital camera, replete with a stuttering series of disconcerting jump-cuts, zooms, rapid pans, and refocusing designed to reinforce the perception of the film being a series of amateur "videographic" takes (which of course, in large part, it could not be). The audience thus is forcibly made aware of watching something more like a home movie, with a pseudo-naiveté that renders it more insistently "authentic" than the spectacle of polished cinematic skill. An aesthetic stake such as this calls to mind that of China's scholar-amateur painters, who for centuries rejected craftsmanship and disdained anything to do with prettiness or sweetness while claiming instead the high ground of "sincerity." If *Suzhou River* is to conclude with a romantic leap, its point of departure is nothing less than an unflattering slice of Chinese reality. This is, simultaneously, a rejection of Chinese cinema's "Fifth Generation" style (which, by capturing in traditional "painterly" terms the "unchanging" look of a mythic past, was designed to explore the "essence" of Chinese ways as a basis for exploring China's unchanging authoritarianism) in favor of a high-speed, grainy, raggedy postmodern look. Like many of the serious films of the later 1990s, the turn here is also away from the Fifth Generation's mnemonic fixation on Communist China's past tragedies and toward a focus on the vagaries of the urban present, capturing the compromised realities of daily life as if experienced through some natural or documentary encounter rather than by artificial design.[28] Many of the figures seen along the Suzhou River now turn naturally to the camera, and some even wave (fig. 15), as if to validate the film's "reality" in the here-and-now and lend their own reality—even an intimacy—to a cinematic narrative that is set forth with a "this-*really*-happened-to-me" kind of presence. The intentionally "flawed" visual texture of *Suzhou River* keeps the audience on edge as it holds the film's flawed "heroes" at arm's length from any false heroism. As the underlying theme

15   *Suzhou River,* Wave at the Camera

of the film concerns deceit and credibility, *Suzhou River* is at pains to establish its own bona fides with the audience.

Like the first part of *Vertigo,* the first section of *Suzhou River* ends with an apparently fatal fall. *Vertigo*'s fall from a tower is translated into the leap from a bridge into Shanghai's infamous backwater (figs. 16 and 17), but *Suzhou River* is by no means a direct translation of Hitchcock. Unlike Hitchcock's acrophobic Scottie, Mada suffers no parallel fear of drowning, and whereas Scottie fails to make it up the tower steps at San Juan Bautista, Mada manages a brave if futile leap from the bridge after the young

16   *Vertigo,* The Fall

17   *Suzhou River,* The Leap

18   *Suzhou River*, The Mermaid

19   *Suzhou River*, Suzhou River with Garden Bridge

Mudan, who has plunged into Suzhou River. Although he comes up empty-handed, Mada's transforming quest begins here, and here the two films begin significantly to diverge. A second cue to *Suzhou River*'s more idealistic trajectory lies in the heroine's "reincarnation." *Vertigo*'s reincarnate, Judy (Kim Novak), is cast as a rather slutty "broad" (Hitchcock makes much of her "animal-like sensuality" and "the fact that she wears no brassiere"[29]), and she requires nothing less from Jimmy Stewart than a complete makeover in order to restore her original allure. *Suzhou River*'s Meimei, on the other hand, is contrasted with the young Mudan in being all grown up now, more beautiful and more seductive than before—a remarkable makeover not only in looks but in every detail of motion and emotion by actress Zhou Xun. But more alluring still is Meimei's professional persona as a blond-haired mermaid, living on a houseboat by day and swimming about in an oversized fish bowl by night (fig. 18). *Suzhou River* might have been set anywhere—high up a mountain or elsewhere on dry land—but for the central vehicle of the mermaid (*meirennü*). Ontologically, the mermaid dictates that there be a river, not the other way around. The videographer's anthropological introduction to the people of Suzhou River ("There's a century worth of stories here and rubbish," he says at the outset of the film, "which make it Shanghai's dirtiest river. I will show you families and love and loneliness. . . .") exists primarily in anticipation of the mermaid's full-blown appearance in part two (fig. 19). The reappearance of actress Zhou Xun as a lovely mermaid is formally the film's most striking MacGuffin, as misleading to our detective instincts as it is fascinating.

Cinematically, the way for this putative linkage between Mudan and Meimei is paved early on when Mada gives Mudan a mermaid doll on her birthday, the day her affection for him first blossoms openly (fig. 20; *Suzhou River* DVD, Scene 2). The relationship that it betokens is hardly symmetrical, and the little mermaid serves as a visual marker of the sexual allure that distances the adolescent girl from the mature target of her affection. For Mudan, the doll becomes a sexualized fetish upon which she showers her attention, a fantasy self and an image of the creature she hopes to grow up to be in order to fully claim Mada's affections. Stricken by Mada's betrayal, when Mudan

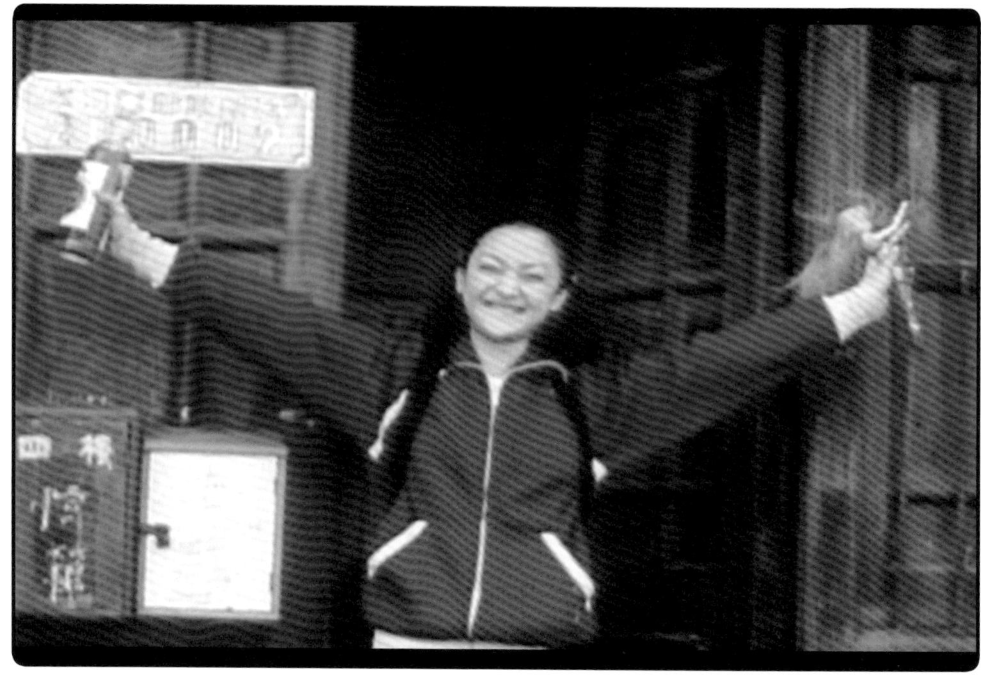

Suzhou River, Birthday Doll

plunges into Suzhou River with doll in hand, she vows to "turn into a mermaid and come looking for you" (fig. 17). The pose recalls Mudan's initial appearance with the doll (fig. 20). And when Mudan seems to come back later reincarnated as Meimei, it seems that she comes to life as the doll as well. Scenes of the mature Meimei in her black underwear preparing to appear as the mermaid resonate with remembered scenes of little Mudan in her underwear, childishly—but with hints of her sexual precocity—playing with her doll (figs. 21 and 22). The fact that Meimei's mermaid act is set as a come-on to patrons in the same "Love Bar" where Mada had taken Mudan on her

Suzhou River, Mermaid Dressing

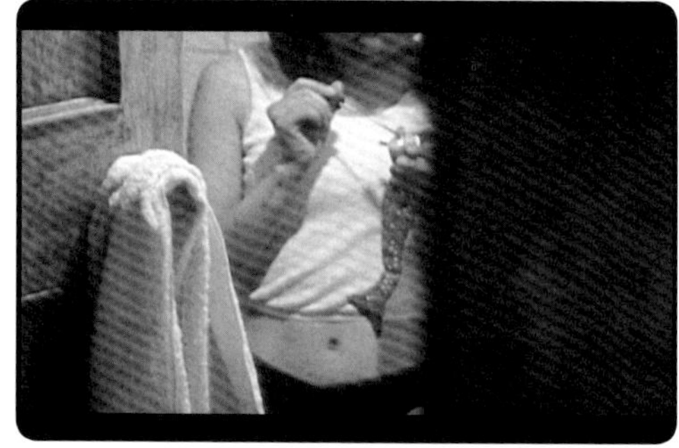

Suzhou River, Doll Play

birthday but also where Mada plotted Mudan's kidnapping not only salutes the quirk-
iness of fate but overdetermines the tragic consequences that will ultimately flow from
such a flawed mixture of motives. Toward the end, an ambiguous figure resembles
Meimei with hair up in pigtails like Mudan as she sings a song about "breaking up"
and "letting go" (fig. 48).

If *Suzhou River*'s application of Western *film noir* to Shanghai extends a century-
long dialogue about the semi-Western nature of China's model "modern" town, this
Barbie doll of a mermaid extends the reference to modern Chinese hybridity still
further—a corporate-manufactured female body as a determinant of public ideals, complete with blond hair and a red-sequined bikini bra. Even though various fish-men
and fish-women can be found with passing reference in Chinese mythological lore,[30]
Lou Ye remembers his parents introducing him to Hans Christian Andersen's "The
Little Mermaid" as a child and readily acknowledges that "the whole idea [of the
mermaid] is a Western import, like Coca-Cola and McDonald's—like everything Fifth
Generation filmmakers refused to admit as Chinese." "This, I think, is a very important difference with filmmakers of my generation. We're not interested in being
cultural immigration officials saying, this is Chinese, this is not Chinese."[31] But while
the Western myth of the mermaid stretches back to Roman times, neither Andersen
nor traditional Western lore can fully illuminate the range of associations this image
carries for a Chinese audience. None of the Western precedents invokes the death-and-
resurrection essential to the putative disappearance-and-reappearance of Mudan as
Meimei. Hans Christian Andersen's "Little Mermaid" has great cachet in China these
days, but despite its elements of women and water, love and beauty, fidelity and pursuit, mistaken identity and transfiguration, and sublimation of love into spiritual quest,
there is no confusion in Andersen of the living with the dead, and no parallel to *Suzhou
River*'s repeated transformations of pursued into pursuer: Mada pursued by Mudan
then obsessed by her romantic innocence, Meimei pursued by Mada then taking up
his obsession.[32] More illuminating of the mythic dimensions at play here is a cluster
of Chinese traditions that link female beauty with water, water with marriage-and-
sacrifice or love-and-suicide, and these with a corporeal return-from-the-dead.

Throughout much of Chinese recorded history, in times of flood, to right the
imbalance between *yin* and *yang*, beautiful young females were offered up as "brides"
to pacify the angry gods of the river in rituals led by local priests. The famous final
scene of the film *Yellow Earth* (1985) accurately records a related ceremony as con-
ducted in northern Shaanxi, with the female sacrifice cast cinematically in the form of
an accident that is then sublimated into the submergence of a hollow ceramic vessel.[33]
(Drought, by contrast, brought about by an excess of *yang*, was fought by exposing
young males to death on a mountainside beneath a glaring sun.) This "marital" drowning had its closest parallel in the unhappy outcome of forbidden love[34] and matchless
loyalty, or the conspicuous absence of these in the case of unloved wives.[35] Suicide by
drowning amongst Chinese women as a statistically massive phenomenon has always

been inflated by the historic traditions of arranged marriage and exogamy (whereby marriage removes females from their family and their native village), and even after the reduction of these to a largely rural practice in recent times, Chinese female suicides remain about a quarter of all the world's suicides.[36] Mao Zedong, whose first rebellion was against his own arranged marriage, was preoccupied early on by the subject, and Chinese cinematic tradition is rich in reference to such events, from the several films made of Ba Jin's *Family* (1941, 1953, 1956) through *Woman from the Lake of Scented Souls* (1992).[37] The female suicidal act was typically achieved by a desperate leap into the local river or lake or, if vengeance was part of the equation, by polluting the family well or garden pond, thus assuring that the unhappy spirit of the drowned girl could continue to haunt the family courtyard and drive away guests. In addition to such suicides were the distinguished suicides by drowning out of loyalty to a deceased husband, following the legendary model of the two wives of Emperor Shun, the Goddess and Lady of the Xiang River.[38] Now to the point: in China's nature lore, so many of the deified spirits of lakes and rivers were the victims of such suicides that even today, a Chinese audience watching Mudan plunge into Suzhou River might regard the event as perfectly "natural"; and the audience might equally well anticipate her return in some incarnate form or another.

It is among these spirits—beautiful, haunted, drowned women—that we must seek the origins of *Suzhou River*'s mermaid. The beautiful spirit of the Luo River was often seen in paintings that illustrated the rhapsodic poem (*fu*) by the Wei-dynasty prince Cao Zhi (192–232), whose literary conceits were that in his travels along the banks of the Luo, none but his charioteer could see and describe this lovely phantasm (fig. 23), and that his goddess was a subject of painting even before the poem put her description into words:

> In her a balance is struck between plump and frail,
> A measured accord between diminutive and tall,
> With shoulders shaped as if by carving,
> Waist narrow as though bound with white cords;
> At her slim throat and curving neck
> The pale flesh lies open to view, . . .
> Cloud-bank coiffeur rising steeply,
> Long eyebrows delicately arched,
> Red lips that shed their light abroad,
> White teeth gleaming within,
> Bright eyes skilled at glances,
> A dimple to round off the base of the cheek—
> Her rare form wonderfully enchanting,
> Her manner quiet, her pose demure. . . .
> Her face and figure live up to her paintings. . . .[39]

23 Gu Kaizhi, attributed, *Spirit of the Luo River*, detail, original ca. 400. Palace Museum, Beijing (from *Zhongguo meishu quanji* 1)

Perhaps there is something of Barbie in this description, ancient as it may be. More importantly, like *Suzhou River*, the poem is all about faith, or the lack of it. In seducing the poet, the river spirit invites the poet to pursue her—where else?—to an underwater tryst: committing himself, in other words, forever. But he lacks the courage. A love-suicide is not for him, not even with a revived female suicide, but like Mada, once Mudan has disappeared into the depths, the poet realizes his error and redoubles his pursuit. It is not that Lou Ye has *this* poem in mind, but such tales of one-time opportunities thoughtlessly lost and then vigorously pursued form the backbone of Chinese romantic lore.[40] The Luo River poem's finale includes a lament by the goddess that unlike in ages past, in *this* faithless age men and gods must now live far apart (shades of modern anomie some eighteen hundred years ago; substitute a blond mermaid in this modern myth for the ancient river goddess).

All in all, whether done in by sacrifice or suicide, female water-spirits were typically associated with the issue of fidelity and return. And women, not men, were the ones with the courage—or desperation—to "take the plunge." Thus, when Mudan leaps from the bridge, it is not quite a suicide: not only does she not die, nor does she seem mature enough to fully comprehend her own possible demise, but she plunges in with the (culture-bound) faith that her transit will be momentary, leading to her immanent "return." Impervious to death itself, she is focused only on returning to punish Mada, or to seduce him, or both. Clearly, then, this blond mermaid suggests a multiple hybridity, not just the conjunction of man and animal (woman and fish, that is) but of West and East as well. What might prove most surprising to the Chinese audience is that none of the culturally predictable events ever come to pass, that Meimei isn't Mudan after all, that Mudan doesn't come back with fish scales to haunt Mada, having never died in the first place. *Suzhou River*, after all, is more surprising, more

mysterious than that. It is a Chinese ghost story without a ghost—at least not until
the last act, with the belated death of Mudan. But that act, too, is foretold by the
cinematic image.

When Mada and Mudan come together again briefly, they sit facing the sunset. She
looks upward, hopeful; his expression is upward first, then downcast. As the camera
shifts from an equal focus on the two of them to one primarily on her, it is evident
that he is but the messenger, she is the message, and that he is now expendable, as is
their union (fig. 24). In between these two views of the couple, we see, as they do, the
famous Oriental Pearl Tower rising across the Huangpu River from the Garden Bridge
in Shanghai's recently emergent Pudong district (figs. 25 and 26). Completed in 1995
at 468 meters in height, with a conference hall at 350 meters, a restaurant and disco
hall at 267 meters, and hotel rooms below, it is currently Asia's tallest television
tower and the third tallest tower in the world, decorated by two large and nine small
spheres resembling pearls (with hotel suites inside). It is a scramble of imagery and
eras, most obviously a symbol of Shanghai's dream of a Disneyland future. Like so
many of China's recent high-rise buildings that hitch the promise of a dazzling, ven-
turistic economic future to a stabilizing pride in China's cultural heritage, its formal

24 *Suzhou River*, Reunion

25 *Suzhou River*, Reunion with Towe

26 *Suzhou River*, Oriental Pearl Tower

design also derives from Buddhist pagodas of the past: multistoried icons of worldly renunciation whose pearl-decorated finials symbolize transcendental wisdom (figs. 27 and 28). Like the pagoda, Shanghai's Oriental Pearl Tower encompasses a dream world, a mighty transformation from the mundane and the ordinary; but through the transforming agencies of modern materialism and nationalistic longings, its difference from a *real* pagoda measures New China's distance from its cultural roots: here is a modern world where nostalgia is largely disengaged from any deep understanding of the past for which it longs and which operates, instead, as a kind of free-floating alienation from the unspirited and desacralized present. It is a scornful world in which the search for spiritual significance stigmatizes and further isolates the already isolated. If the lowly couple is merely dreaming of a romantic night together in an elegant, elevated suite complete with turn-down bed service—that is, of becoming part of Shanghai's, and China's, beckoning economic future—we cannot tell. The sexual potency of this upright image might strike a Western audience as obvious symbolism, but the imagery is more resonant than that. Emblematic of the Buddha's spiritual quest achieved, of his death, burial, and final departure from this world, of karmic transmission and the passing on of his quest to others, the pagoda is a reminder that Mada's mission also is done and his fate is now sealed. The Oriental Pearl Tower served as a backdrop for Mudan's plunge from the Garden Bridge. Now, a culturally informed audience might well see Mada's death unfolding before it actually transpires on film: no sooner is Mada's ideal woman recaptured than his departure from this world is immanent, inevitable. Death is the only possible outcome: spiritually, psychologically, and cinematically, not as a tragedy but as a necessary fulfillment of the narrative. Mada is primarily a dreamer, and it is not his purpose to live out his life with a *real* female by his side. From this point on, there *are* ghosts, not one but two of them. What happens next is a tale of China's destiny.

Shanghai's Oriental Pearl Tower is *Suzhou River*'s cinematic reply to *Vertigo*'s mission tower at San Juan Bautista, the towers as death symbols, a neo-Buddhist icon substituted for a Christian one: death for death, but with a difference. *Vertigo* concludes on a dizzying tragic note of frustrated sexuality, religious intervention, and

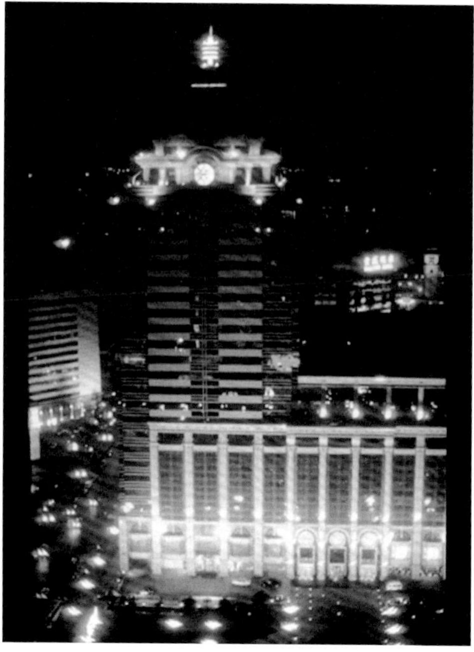

27 Hengji Center at Night, Beijing (author's photo)

28 Great Wild Goose Pagoda, Xi'an, restored 648 (author's photo)

disappearance, cynically exposing the fraudulence of romantic love—very *noir*. *Suzhou River* approaches its conclusion with a reassertion of the romantic ideal, sincere feelings displacing materialist ideology—almost anti-*noir*. What happens after this double-death is more important than what comes before. Next comes the transmission of Mudan's spirit to Meimei. But then, *Suzhou River*'s tale has been told all along by—and its last word will be given to—the *noir*, could-care-less narrator, so that Mudan's high ideals are balanced by muted expectations, as multi- or ambi-valent as the Oriental Pearl Tower image.

By the end of *Vertigo*, the hero has reprised the misdeeds of the villain and is, for the second time around, the agent of the heroine's demise—the first time imagined, but this time for real. The double-disappearance in *Vertigo*, Hitchcock's clever one-upmanship of his own earlier films, becomes a triple-disappearance in *Suzhou River*. Mudan, as it turns out, has long been gone; she is *not* Meimei. Now, with her return, Mada disappears, and the cause of their death for all we can tell is pure fate, a motor-cycle "accident" near the bridge they had jumped from earlier (fig. 29). But it is a meaningful fate, or it has a fated meaning, which requires that the cinematic focus continue shifting to the surviving couple, Meimei and her videographer boyfriend, to see what lesson the second couple will make of all this. It is now, upon *her* learning that Mudan has not come back as Meimei, that the mermaid Meimei determines to reverse this course and to come back as Mudan—by disappearing as Mudan once

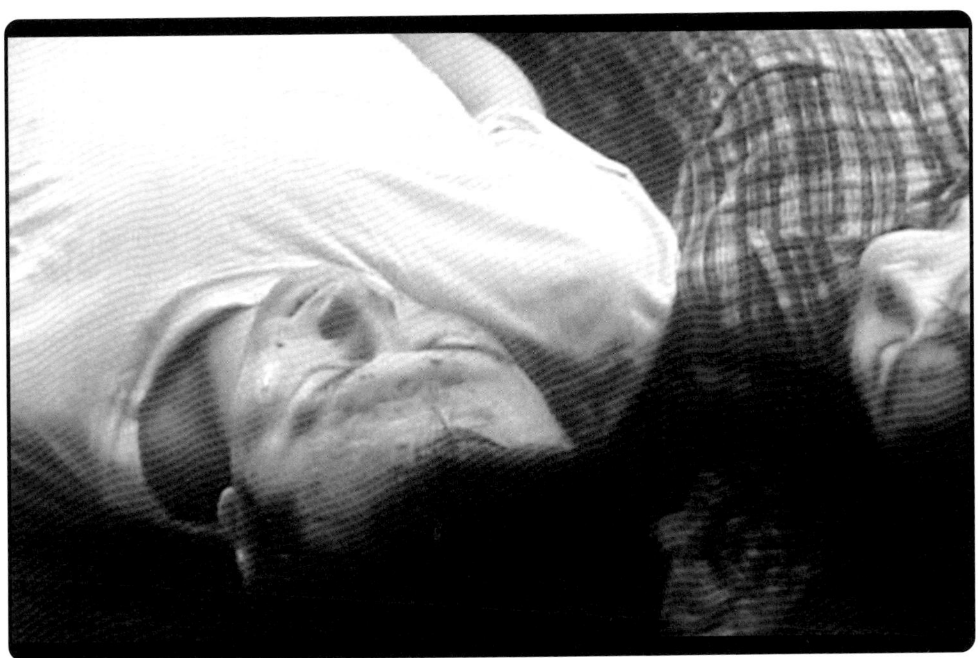

29 *Suzhou River,* Dead Lovers

did, taking the pursuit of an ideal as her reality, and transforming herself into the object of that pursuit. This third disappearance constitutes a radical extension—and in effect, a reversal—of Hitchcock's formula. But this is not the final act, as Lou Ye provides his film with something of a dual ending.

As the unwilling subject of Mada's pursuit, and not convinced of the sincerity of his tale, Meimei is not only horrified at the sight of her near-double lying dead in the rain, but also astounded (fig. 44). "I didn't think Mudan really existed!" she mutters afterwards. "I thought it was just a story. . . . I thought it was me he wanted. . . ." Each of the characters having already been defined by their swimming or their diving moments, now the pouring rain unites them. Mada's death immediately becomes for Meimei a martyrdom, a transfiguration, a revelation. "He never lied," she murmurs to herself. "Never. . . . Things like that happen only in love stories." "If I left you," Meimei now challenges her videographer boyfriend, "would you pursue me? . . . Would you pursue me forever?" (fig. 30). The first time these questions were asked in the film, at the very beginning, they were heard in total darkness, with the audience not knowing who asks them or why[41] (fig. 47). The words constitute a riddle whose explication the film runs its entire length to provide. Following a bracketing structure common in Chinese storytelling, painting, and cinema and playing strongly to audience expectations, an answer *must* come back at some point, closing the frame that was opened up by the question, and doing so once again in darkness.[42] Again, to the videographer's easy reply, "Yes," Meimei responds, "You're lying," and now she

30 *Suzhou River*, "If I left you . . . "

disappears into the darkness to test his resolve. Ironically, up to this point in the narrative, the videographer has been shown as a strict recorder of the truth, even to the point of callousness. Yet she he has trusted him—entrusted herself, her image, to him, even played the narcissist. But by now, having witnessed true devotion for the first time, she grasps the limitations, the insincerity and even the *self*-deception (on both his part and hers) of their mutual attachment.

In turning from one couple to the next, Lou Ye emphasizes less the puzzle of *personal* identity (which is now settled but which doesn't settle the thematic tensions of the film) than the underlying theme of fidelity, pursuit, and redemption—that is, the constituents of *moral* identity. At first, Lou turns away from Hitchcock's emphasis on the corrosive manipulation of the heroine by the hero and instead toward the steadfast determination and lofty purpose that drives the heroic quest. The self-confident Meimei sublimates the Hitchcockian phenomenon of disappearance-as-criminal-outcome into an act of *social* commitment (could this *not* be a public metaphor?), transforms symptom into cause, victimhood into control, and converts loss, regret, and impotence into opportunity and hope for the future.

Here sublimation leads back to its own source in allegory, to its own inspiration through the discovery of meaning, which is precisely the experience that Meimei undergoes in this film. Just as the innocent, romantic Mudan is perceived by Meimei as representing something more than just another lost child, Mada's corruption partakes in

Shanghai's—and China's—corruption, in an age where unfettered materialism and perversion of official ideology run all the way from the backwaters of Suzhou Creek to the government offices in Beijing. Corruption, the *perception* of which now helps to define daily life in the New China, has left no one behind in the wake of ideological decline. As much in the public imagination as in reality, the void created in this "worker's paradise" by ideological disintegration and economic decentralization is now filled by nineteenth-century-style sweatshops, entrepreneurship manipulated (rather than regulated) from on high, and Party "kleptocracy." Popular jingles spare no one in skewering the decline of values and widespread corruption of today:

> Officials are addicted to money
> While the people labor and sweat.
> If something else counts, then it's funny
> That no one's run into it yet.[43]

"Even if someone [who's an official] doesn't want to be corrupt, it's really hard," runs a popular complaint. "People will still make demands on him since he has power." "If someone is righteous, what use is it? . . . She or he ends up on the bottom."[44] Just how systematic corruption has become in post-Mao China is suggested by Richard Levy:

> Popular thinking about corruption is thus a bundle of contradictions. On the one hand, there is deep anger about corruption, a profound suspicion of those in power, and a willingness to believe the most scandalous tales about China's elites. Moreover, there is an awareness that corruption pervades the whole system. Yet corruption is seen as inevitable and as part of a system that has brought more positive benefits than negative liabilities. Attention is directed more toward how to get along in a corrupt world and how, if possible, to benefit from it than to change it. There is little realistic hope of fundamentally rooting out corruption.[45]

Just as a persistent criminality lent American *film noir* an existential despair in the years when the hard-won victories over the Great Depression and German totalitarianism gave way to stalemate in the Cold War,[46] criminality and corruption in *Suzhou River* come at a time when modern China's loftiest hopes for social and moral reform have fallen by way of repeated Maoist deceits and the post-Mao phenomenon of "jumping into the sea" of free market capitalization. The abandonment of Mudan by her bootlegging father and her kidnapping by Mada and his corrupt friends parallel the kidnapping of public innocence; and these signifiers raise the question of whether Mudan's innocent affection, Mada's unusual acknowledgment of guilt and his obsessive pursuit of redemption, and Meimei's conversion to an ecstatic vision of fidelity serve as inspiration for others or as alternatives to China's public cynicism. In other words, is the artistry of *Suzhou River* or anything like it capable of producing an uplifting social impact? Is it really less *noir* than it is anti-*noir*? Or will the audience remain transfixed in its cynicism, like the videographer, deceiving no one but themselves? Such questions, of course, do not precipitate an answer; like Meimei's challenge to her uncomprehending videographer boyfriend, they really demand *no* answer—not verbally anyway: doubting words, and reaching beyond images and illusions, they represent a call to *action*. At this point, it starts to become clear that the film is less interested in the narrative than in questions of narration.

It is only with the shift of focus from the first couple to the second that Lou Ye clarifies the real thrust of his film, a shift from the structured tension between Mada and the others (Mudan, Meimei, and the videographer) to that between Meimei (who internalizes the values of Mada and Mudan) and the videographer (who does not). This directs our attention, in the end, to another theme, that of voyeurism— which in *Vertigo* defined the emasculated Scottie's "play" with Judy and which played out so fatally in *Rear Window*, *Psycho*, and other Hitchcock films. In *Suzhou River*, voyeurism is an even deeper indicator than bootlegging and kidnapping of China's moral malaise. Earlier scenes of Mada's nightly viewing of videotapes (of music or pornography, one cannot quite tell) and his passivity about *real* women first introduce this theme (fig. 31), and his subsequent spying on Meimei in her dressing room continues the practice. But obsessive spectatorship is even more strongly attached to *Suzhou River*'s videographer-narrator, so withdrawn from the center of events that he is never even named and, but for an occasional hand or leg poking forward from his camera (and one distant glimpse from behind as he delivers Meimei to her houseboat), remains virtually unseen (figs. 32 and 46). Much of the film (all of it, theoretically) has been witnessed through the videographer's own camera—a film within a film, purportedly—and much of it is told through his voice. Indirectly then, he presents the

31 *Suzhou River*, Mada as Voyeur

32 *Suzhou River*, The Voyeur's Meimei

33 *Rear Window*, Hitchcock on Set

real filmmaker Lou Ye's reflection on the passive-aggressive qualities of his medium, and one cannot help but wonder whether Lou Ye actually *played* this role, unattributed in the credits. (Hitchcock's own habitual brief appearances in his own films similarly nod in that direction [fig. 33].) Only gradually and belatedly is the audience led to realize that this seemingly detached and passive narrative—a quaint and wandering tale that this nameless character has picked up somewhere in his graphic wanderings up and down Suzhou River, punctuated with a great many narrative pauses and "now what-ifs," as if he were making it up as he goes and could not commit himself to a determinative reality—is his own confessional. But the story, after meandering like a creek, eventually develops a force of its own with a boomerang-like trajectory that gets away from the videographer and thoroughly ensnares him in the end. It becomes his own story, too, as his fate becomes entangled with that of Mada and the multiple female targets, real and imagined, of Mada's conflicted pursuits. Seeking only to peep vicariously into the lives of others and not to wander out from behind his camera, the vulnerability of the videographer to the events that slowly unfold around him is wholly unintentional and unexpected. When Mada confronts the videographer with his tale, for example, the camera remains fixed between them. And when the videographer wants Mada confronted—beaten up—for horning in on his woman, he has someone else (the bouncers at Meimei's bar) do it for him. But by the end, like it or not, he has become a primary participant in the tale. And yet by that point he has retreated again even farther behind his lens, which forces us to realize that here is one more example—indeed, the prime example—of the inability to commit oneself romantically. And this is why (like the Luo River poet) he tells this tale as a lament over failed romance: succeed, live out the romance, and the tale need not be told.

The videographer's fetish for graphic appropriation (which forms such a contrast with his own near invisibility, but that is the mark of the true voyeur) is synonymous here with the film director's own cinematic craft and has been evident from the beginning of the film, which parallels Hitchcock's obsession with local detail. Although he much preferred studio-based production, for *Vertigo* Hitchcock made extensive studies of the Mission Dolores, the Lombard District, Powell Street, the Legion of Honor, Fort Point, San Juan Bautista, and Big Basin, all shown at particular times of day and seasonal conditions. Lou Ye was equally possessed about Suzhou River, that man-made canal between Suzhou and Shanghai better known in English by the less attractive name "Suzhou Creek" and best known by what it is not: it is not Shanghai's glamorous front door, the Huangpu River with its famous Bund built in the 1930s and its burgeoning Pudong district built in the 1990s and still going up, a river lined with Asia's biggest banks and tallest office buildings from two eras. Rather, it is Shanghai's back door, dating back to the time when Shanghai was dominated by foreign concessions and the Chabei district just north of the creek was the world's busiest "Chinatown." This warehouse district, as seedy as its image here on tape is

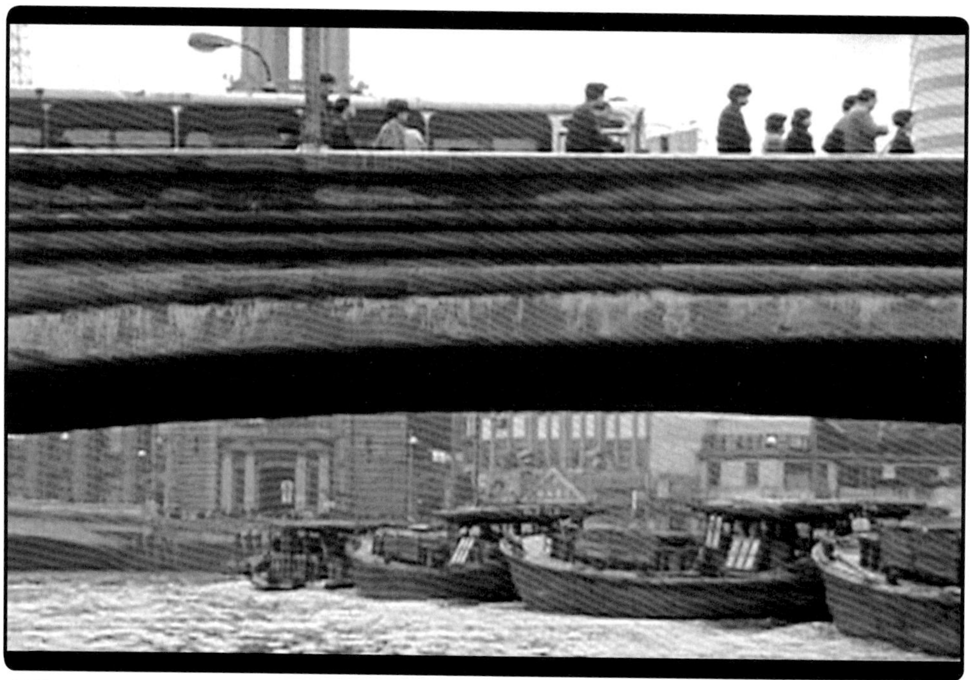

34 *Suzhou River, Bridge*

   HITCHCOCK WITH A CHINESE FACE

grainy, is home to the hardworking, home to fishermen and boat people who scarcely ever leave the water, home to Shanghai's bootleggers, smugglers, and petty criminals, to the wharves and the nightclubs that hug the shore (fig. 34; *Suzhou River* DVD, Scene 1). These are classic *film noir* walk-ons in a classic *noir* setting, narrated with the classic I-lost-it-all despondency of *film noir* voice-overs: "If you watch it long enough, the river will show you everything," the videographer obsesses at the outset, and indeed he does watch it long and hard. Hitchcock would probably have loved the detailed graphing of this polluted river with its vibrant inhabitants, but ultimately this framing becomes the basis for moral concern. Although the videographer-narrator himself is never quite seen by the audience, persistently refusing to abandon his end of the lens or his own point of view (only hands or legs appear on occasion), it is precisely this constrained viewpoint that by the end of the film becomes the chief object of scrutiny.

Daily life in China might now be somewhat free of mass campaigns, but it is hardly free of the cynicism that inspires them. The grand analogy of *Suzhou River* is even closer to the obsessive voyeurism of *Rear Window*'s Jeffries (Jimmy Stewart) (fig. 35) than to *Vertigo*, an analog borrowed from filmmaking itself that reflects on the art of appropriation. It reaches deep into the politics of daily life and the daily life of politics, which in China are entwined with the filmic/recording process. It might be read as this: that the goal of surveillance is collective conformity; that the Chinese public

35   *Rear Window*, Hooked on Looking

36   *Suzhou River*, Rear Windows   37   *Suzhou River*, Meimei on Tape

has been circumscribed for so long by public surveillance—historically by the family, ranging from parents and grandparents to clan councils, and in modern times by the state through its techniques and technology of surveillance[47]—that, even with political decentralization and the relative degree of personal freedom of the present decade, citizens of the People's Republic have little experience or expectation of individual privacy. Daily life in China remains tightly circumscribed by habit and scripted by residual government scrutiny. Hong Kong films like Wong Kar-Wai's *Chungking Express* (1994) and Taiwan films beginning with Tsai Ming-liang's *Rebels of the Neon God* (1992) seem to equate modern apartment living not only with personal alienation but with the colonial isolation and the otherness that envelops those societies. In *Suzhou River*, by contrast, everything from morning tooth brushing to family fights is carried out on apartment balconies and the roofs of riverboats for all to see and for the camera of the film's videographer to record (fig. 36; *Suzhou River* DVD, Scene 1). But Lou Ye seems to suggest that in order to participate in a more meaningful life, in order for personal life to absorb the freedoms and confront the challenges of "modernity," one must declare an individuality, reject collective authority, and step away from the public view—one must step away from the camera (a device of the collective gaze), throw away the script, and seize upon life's more dramatic possibilities. Real life, in other words, should be less like the manipulative process of filmmaking and more like the fantasy of freedom that movies project—not caught up in the staging of the thing but reaching out toward the possibilities that cinema extends. Read backwards: the deadliest foe of romantic faith and the silent co-conspirator of social corruption is seen as public passivity, conditioned by decades and centuries of surveillance and its co-option of personal agency. The videographer is a "postsocialist" man, the first generation of Chinese for whom the modern tools of government surveillance have fallen into private hands; but while he may be a professional, an entrepreneur in pursuit of profit, like the government he knows too well he sets about compulsively spying on his friends and neighbors, amateurishly and destructively. Read ironically: this is a film that indicts its own filmic process; at the same time as it depicts the strategies of innocence, it seems to enter a guilty plea. If the state's surveillance is a kind of thievery, stealing the citizens' privacy, then this stealing of the state's own methods of stealing is like crawling into a den of thieves to practice a kind of meta-thievery, an appropriative critique that is perhaps innocent by way of intent but morally complicit in its means.

Although he is a solo entrepreneur operating in an aggressively commercial sphere (he is first seen, or at least his arms are, spray-painting an ad for his services and his telephone number on a warehouse wall), *Suzhou River*'s videographer preserves the unregenerate attitude of surveillant statecraft. "I'll shoot anything," he says of his fetish for the camera, in his own self-introduction. "Weddings, birthdays, I'll even shoot you pissing or making love. . . . But don't complain if you don't like what you see." The videographer tells a certain truth, but a harsh and cynical one. His work and his pleasures are emblematic of China's prioritization of the public ahead of the private and are a counterpart to the state's own dominant ideology, its staging of public spectacles, its co-option of individuals and individuality, its rendering every private act a public one. His favorite activity is *capturing* his girlfriend Meimei on tape, manipulating her more subtly but ultimately just as callously as Mada kidnaps Mudan. "I didn't know anything about Meimei's past," he narrates. "She didn't say, and I never asked. I just liked to look at her and video her" (fig. 37). The ultimate target of surveillance is public criticism of public authority, and its ultimate goal is the establishment of a compliant passivity. Meimei's submission to the camera throughout most of the film is a reminder of the readiness of a captive public to negotiate an acceptable subalternity with its captor; her narcissism plays all too well to his vicarious urge. She is forever seen through glass: her make-up mirror (fig. 38), the transparent aquarium where she exhibits herself to the public eye, the camera lens through which she exhibits herself for her boyfriend. Her visuality is highlighted, but at the same time it is contested by her periodic disappearances from her videographer-boyfriend's view, most emphatically at the climax of the film when she unilaterally breaches the voyeuristic-narcissist contract and departs from the scene—an event which appropriately goes unseen and unrecorded by the videographer or by the film itself, which records only the trace of her departure in a note left behind: "Come and find me!"

"Cameras don't lie," the videographer declares at the end of his introductory soliloquy, but we know better. Cameras, like words, can deceive; images are forged and reconstructed, and even when not falsified visually, they are put to all kinds of uses and abuses, made to lie in any number of ways.[48] *Suzhou River* is all about the interaction of truth and deception, reality and illusion, and the camera can provide both. In one of the film's most intensely visual moments, Mudan in captivity is asked by Mada to sing over the telephone for her father to confirm her identity. She begins to

38   *Suzhou River*, The Mermaid's Mirror

sing a song of her love and loyalty for Mada, learned in his apartment: "your face always appears in my dreams." But it is *her* face that appears and her expression that slowly changes over the forty-five seconds of silence that follow. Her confusion about the purpose of this singing turns visibly into suspicion then into a perceptible recognition of Mada's betrayal as she slowly turns to look *at him* and finally reflects a face of resentment (figs. 39 and 40). This scene is shortly afterwards followed by a thirty-second shot showing Mada's fellow kidnapper Xiao Hong. Her expression turns from joy (shouting "We're rich!" as she recovers the ransom money), to the sudden

39   *Suzhou River*, Mudan Betrayed, I

40   *Suzhou River*, Mudan Betrayed, II

41 *Suzhou River*, Xiao Hong Betrayed, I

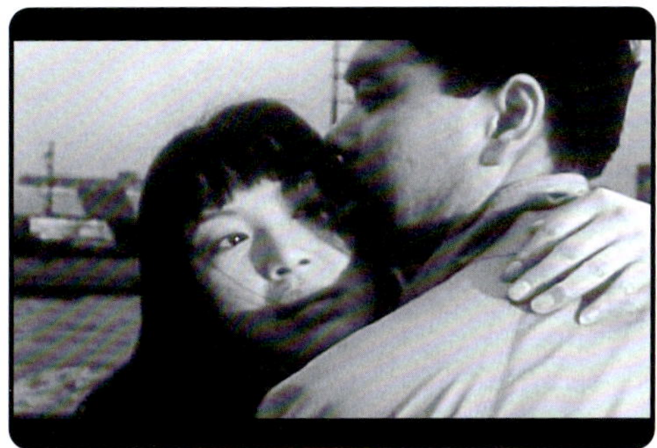

42 *Suzhou River*, Xiao Hong Betrayed, II

43 *Suzhou River*, Xiao Hong Betrayed, III

44 *Suzhou River*, Meimei as Witness

awareness of a new, unanticipated reality, to coughing up blood as she in turn is betrayed by the third party to the kidnap plot, Lao B.—rushing to hug him but impaling herself instead on his unseen weapon (figs. 41–43). In these scenes, the camera accurately provides a record of deceit, but it can also offer its own deceptions. In its own ironic honesty, *Suzhou River* does not hesitate even to target itself; while self-introduced as if narrated and shot by the videographer as a film-within-a-film, a determined viewing can easily locate the breakdown of this structure and isolate the many passages which don't match that artistic conceit (beginning with our first introduction to the young Mudan in the same time frame and panning sequence in which the videographer has been busily tracking Meimei's comings and goings from his balcony). Another revelation of the film's conceit/deceit occurs when Mada dies, and Meimei (in the rain, like a grounded mermaid) sees her own double for the first time, lying dead by Mada's side: she turns directly to the camera, as if it were able to show her some much-needed truth about how this could be (fig. 44). But this becomes the very moment when she first realizes that Mada all along has had the greater truth to offer—"He never lied," she says—and a rebellious vision is generated of a different world that *could* be, a world without deception. Image itself is challenged: what Mada wanted in Meimei was *not* her heavily commodified, flashy mermaid surface but the innocent, affectionate, needy child within. To the passive-aggressive videographer, then, when he proclaims his readiness to make a similar romantic leap of faith ("Would you pursue me?" "Yes."), she knowingly replies, "You're lying."

Clearly, though, it is more than just the videographic process that is dismantled here. Words, images, slogans, propaganda, materialism, and cynicism are all indicted for their lack of sincerity, which lurks deep within the human heart. Throughout the film, the videographer's frequent narrative hesitations and uncertainties about where the story might go next not only hint that the film's many riverine twists and rhetorical turns are perhaps opportunistic fabrications designed to favor the narrator's own cause, but also reflect his own weak attachment to objective reality and therefore challenge his assertion early in the film that "photographs don't lie." Mostly they parallel his vicarious orientation and lack of true emotional commitment:

A boy and a girl who hardly know each other sit next to each other. What happens next? [Pause.] Well [long pause, change of scene], love, of course (fig. 45; *Suzhou River* DVD, Scene 2).

45   *Suzhou River, Love, of Course*

Or the story was not as romantic as imagination, is not so simple. There's more to it. Maybe Mada's not simply a courier. What if Xiao Hong has some criminal connections? And what if she and Mada had been lovers?

And then? That's the end, I suppose. Not much of a love story . . . but I don't know [the film fades almost to blackness] how to go on with it. Unless . . . [the light and color slowly return] Mada can finish telling the story himself.

Undone by Meimei's challenge, the videographer's final comment in the film is spoken with a deep, dark cynicism that clearly invites even the audience's distrust. He rejects Meimei's leap to freedom, her conversion to a romantic, individualizing faith, saying, "I could run after her, look for her like Mada . . . and then this love story of mine might go on. But I won't because nothing lasts forever. I'll just take another drink and close my eyes and wait for the next romance to come along" (fig. 46). There is only this much truth in the videographer's final, cynical self-presentation: as he takes "another drink," the camera lurches nauseously; and as he "closes his eyes," the film turns black. This is the darkness with which the film mysteriously began (fig. 47) and now abruptly ends and into which Meimei has plunged in her leap of faith. In it lies the uncertainty and risk that such a leap requires. But preferring image to reality, the videographer is not prepared to go there; and so, he has now lost not only his girlfriend but the only model really worth shooting. This pitch blackness may be the film's most important event, a withholding of that which can be named in truth or accurately shown, a suspension that challenges vicarious experience and questions image-making—even film itself—as an inherently credible medium.

That this "taking a leap" involves a readiness to take some loss is romantically captured late in the film when Meimei begins to merge with Mudan in a scene where one might wonder who is who and never be quite sure. As Meimei retreats from her relationship with the videographer, an ambiguous figure—perhaps one of the videographer's paying clients but with hair pulled up into pigtails like Mudan's and

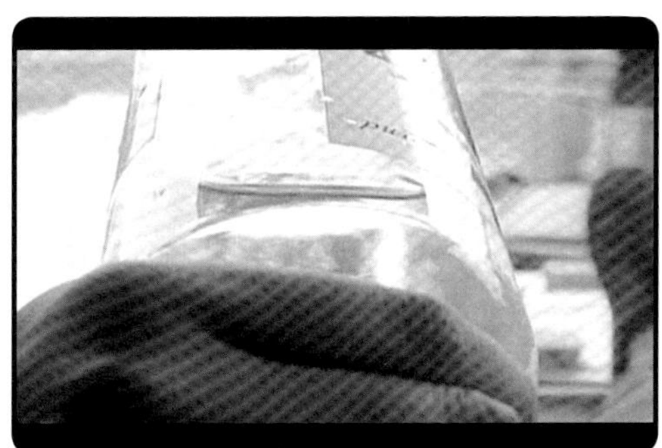

46 *Suzhou River, Another Drink*

47 *Suzhou River, "If I . . ."*

48   *Suzhou River*, *Jietuo*, "Letting Go"

looking even more like Meimei mimicking Mudan's childish ways—with microphone in hand sings the song *Jietuo*, made popular by Taiwan's aboriginal superstar A-Mei, karaoke-style straight into the videographer's camera (fig. 48). The title means "breaking up," "release," "letting go," and even conveys the Daoist sense of "detachment." *Jietuo*, the lyrics say, "means knowing to wipe away old tears, look ahead, / Find new directions toward the future."[49] While the haunting melody issues forth, as it must have many times before in *Suzhou River*'s "Love Bar," a montage of the videographer's work serves as a lament for his loss, seen through the medium he has chosen over his love for Meimei. The montage includes a tearful Meimei whom he is now losing, video-captured memories of his graphic pursuit of her, the videographer's cigarette-holding hands stretched forth from behind his camera over an overflowing ashtray, spray-painting his ads on walls along Suzhou River, and his professional shooting of a wedding, an event that now will never be his and Meimei's thanks to Mada (filmed in the "Love Bar," where the narratives of Mada and the videographer finally collide) and thanks to his own unreadiness to undertake the same risk that Meimei is preparing for (seen last as she applies a paste-on rose tattoo on her left thigh, just as Mudan used to do) (*Suzhou River* DVD, Scene 4). It is the videographer's quintessential moment in which his love for the medium records, appropriates, enfolds, absorbs, and ultimately overpowers his love for his subject. It records both the Meimei he can capture—the fleeting image—and the Meimei he can't keep hold of. For the parting couple, the love song *Jietuo* sings of two different tales: Meimei's letting go of the past and the videographer's letting go of their future.

In the end, it is Mudan whose romance, whose first love and unquestioning devotion, is the model of purity. In one of *Suzhou River*'s greatest departures from Hitchcock's *Vertigo* (not to mention from Freudian views of childhood), it is no accident that the bodyguard's charge is a woman much younger than himself, an immature adolescent intended less to exude sexuality than to convey the spiritual possibilities of innocence. The equation of youth with innocent virtue can be located in many cultural traditions, and one can readily trace its development in Chinese intellectual history. The sixteenth-century philosopher Li Zhi thought that a natural, "childlike state of mind," or *tongxin,* lodged man's innate, inner goodness and that this state of mind, though compromised by social interaction, was still present in the adult. The fourth-century B.C.E. Daoist philosopher Zhuangzi referred ironically to the "stupid" spirit of the newborn calf in order to contrast pure, spontaneous virtue with the compromised knowledge of book learning, which leaves one dependent on authority.[50] Young Mudan embodies that uncompromised sincerity, and it is up to the adults, Mada, Meimei (who, already partially liberated in flights of spontaneity, periodically disappears from the videographer's view), and the videographer himself, to "let go" of their social inhibitions and dependence on authority to discover the remnants of this innocence within themselves.

As a film about film, *Suzhou River* points beyond the back lot to China itself as a kind of cinematic stage, still artificial and carefully manipulating those areas considered most politically sensitive, even while increasingly free in recent decades. One measure of continuing authority and control is the licensing of cinema, with the state still in charge of who can make films (through the Film Bureau) and the Party apparatus totally in charge of which films can be distributed in public movie houses (through the all-powerful China Film Distribution Corporation).[51] In a sense, *Suzhou River* describes the conditions of its own production. Like his videographer, Lou Ye made *Suzhou River* not with film per se but with digital tape. Lou Ye's film grew out of a project licensed for television.[52] It was filmed in 16 mm and—avoiding the elaborate structure of Chinese film censorship—was taken abroad to Germany, where producer Philippe Bober and editor Karl Riedl helped to create a truly global production. As a result, *Suzhou River* has never been cleared for public presentation in China, though Lou Ye expresses some confidence that some day it will be.[53] Ironically, then, the corrupt and controlled situations this film encounters both inside and out sets up the conditions for a leap to freedom, such as Lou Ye and his fictional characters have taken. *Suzhou River* seems less to contest the corruption of Shanghai's working sector than to regard it as a freer, more exciting alternative to the heavy hand of the Maoist era; in fact, it seems even to revel in it as a kind of nostalgic return to the heady era of the 1930s.

Suzhou River, then, opens and closes with unresolved alternatives, represented by the blackness which brackets the film, the blackness that cannot yet be filled in except by the unanswerable question, "If I. . . ?" Represented on the one hand by Mada, Mudan, and Meimei, and on the other hand by the videographer, these alternatives leave us with the unresolvable question: which of these characters best represents China, now and in the future?[54]

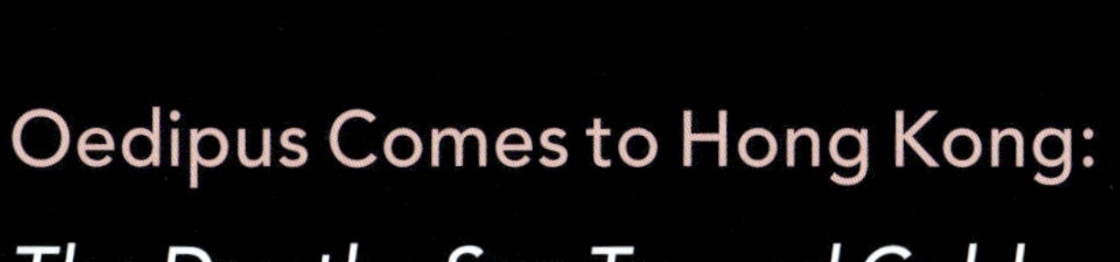

Oedipus Comes to Hong Kong:

The Day the Sun Turned Cold

> If the Oedipus Rex is capable of moving a modern reader or playgoer no less powerfully than it moved the contemporary Greeks, the only possible explanation is that the effect of the Greek tragedy does not depend upon the conflict between fate and human will, but upon the peculiar nature of the material by which this conflict is revealed.
>
> —Sigmund Freud, *The Interpretation of Dreams*

> Parricide, according to a well-known view, is the principal and primal crime of humanity as well as of the individual. It is in any case the main source of the sense of guilt.
>
> —Sigmund Freud, "Dostoevsky and Parricide"

The Day the Sun Turned Cold / Tianguo nizi. Director: Yim Ho; Cinematography: Ho Yung; Film editing: Wong Yee Shun; Music: Otomo Yoshihide, La Bing Zi'ang; Art direction: Jessinta Liu; Cast: Siqin Gaowa (Pu Fengying, mother); Tao Chung Wah (Guan Jian, young man); Shu Zi'ong (Guan Jian, boy); Ma Jingwu (Guan Shichang, father); Wu'ai Zi (Liu Dagui); Li Hu (police captain); Song Yu (Guan Qing, sister); Screenplay: Yim Ho; Original text: Zhang Chenggong ("Ku hai zhong de qiudu" [Swimming through the sea of bitterness]); Production: Yim Ho, Ann Hui; Studio: Chang Chun Television Studio, China Television Joint Production, Dong Xi (Pine East) 1994; 100 minutes

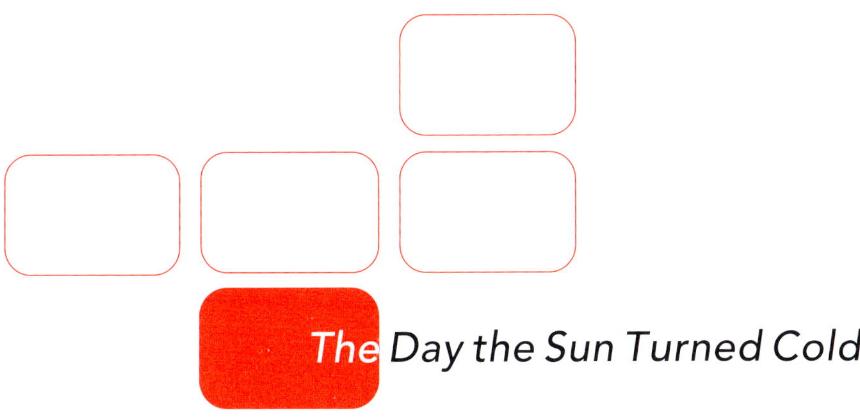

PLOT SUMMARY

This story, as the audience is informed at the outset, is based on actual events. Set in the cold, wintry northeast of China, a young man, Guan Jian, arrives at a police station to report a murder. The victim is his father, he reports, and the murderer is his mother. The murder took place ten years earlier, in 1980. Asked how he came to hate his mother so much, Guan replies calmly that "I don't hate her. She's a good woman and hard working. I love her a lot." The police captain doubts the report and looks into the young man's own background, but finding no problems with him, he begins an interrogation through which the two establish a camaraderie.

In flashback, Guan Jian attempts to recall for the officer scenes from his childhood, beginning with his memories of the cool marital relationship between his father (Guan Shichang, a village school principal, typically stern and often punitive) and his mother (Pu Fengying, an uneducated but warm and nurturing mother). Guan revisits the parents' arguments over how to discipline him for his boyhood delinquencies at school, during which the father throws contempt on his wife's lack of education and disavows his relationship to the boy. One day, in a severe snowstorm, the mother and boy are thrown from their wagon and saved from being buried in a snowbank by a young passing woodcutter, Liu Dagui. This savior is welcomed into the family home by the father and begins a friendship with Pu Fengying. Rumors about their relationship soon begin to circulate among the villagers, climaxing when Guan Jian discovers that Liu Dagui has been to the home in secret and reports this to his father. Guan Shichang gives Pu Fengying a beating and prepares to haul her before the woodcutter, but he immediately suffers a serious attack instead. He fails to recover, and although no cause can be found, Guan Jian recalls seeing his mother mix something strange into his father's food. Years later, after reading of a similar case abroad, he believes this to have been arsenic. Not long afterwards, Guan Shichang dies during a second attack. Pu Fengying, widowed with three dependant children, is soon remarried to Liu Dagui. Guan Jian deeply resents this and refuses to let his siblings move to the new couple's home. A year later, Guan Jian tries to report his father's death as a murder, but this is dismissed as childishness. Pu has a baby girl by Liu, but her relation with him sours, and she returns home to her family. The boy, pleased by her return, sets aside his thoughts of murder.

Now a young man, Guan Jian returns home to demand from Pu Fengying the truth about his father's death. Shocked and angered, she denies his claims and ascribes his doubts to resentment over her remarriage. The police investigation leads to an exhumation of the body, much to the shame of the family, but the results prove negative for the suspected presence of arsenic. Guan begs his mother's forgiveness, and it now appears that Guan has pursued a crime that was never committed, driven by psychological problems in resolving his parental attachments. A restaurant celebration is held to reestablish relations between the son and his family, including Liu Dagui, and a painful forgiveness is extended all around. During this gathering, Liu, in a drunken flashback, imagines asking Pu Fengying to call off their poisoning of her husband, but she instead accuses him of turning his attentions to another woman and refuses. Has Liu merely internalized Guan Jian's fantasies? A short while later, evidence of Guan Shichang's murder through the use of rat poison is confirmed. The couple is arrested, and both are sentenced to death.

Guan Jian, maintaining his usual detached rationality, visits his mother in prison on the eve of her execution, accepting a sweater she has knitted for him in her final hours. On his departure, he throws the sweater into the back of a passing wagon. Liu Dagui's wagon, which ten years earlier saved the mother and child but also led to this tragic pass, is shown as the final image.

As a bicycle rider steers his way through traffic down a busy street, the scene is viewed from the level of the pedals (fig. 49). While the cycle approaches its destination, dodging all obstacles in its way, the parts of the machine go round and round, driving its rider there with an almost palpable mechanical certainty. When the cyclist arrives at his destination, a police station, the wheels seem to have become the fabled wheels of justice, the great Wheel of the Law dispensing karmic retribution. The forward movement is relentless, irreversible. Only later will the audience be in a position to wonder whether the train of events thus set in motion wasn't misdirected, and whether the tragedy unleashed by this journey could not have been stopped.

Each of the three films discussed in this book begins in travel: by boat down a river in *Suzhou River;* by foot through the fields and paddies of Guangdong in *Good Men, Good Women;* by bicycle down the streets of a wintry north Chinese town in *The Day the Sun Turned Cold.* In each of these films, the opening frames reveal the

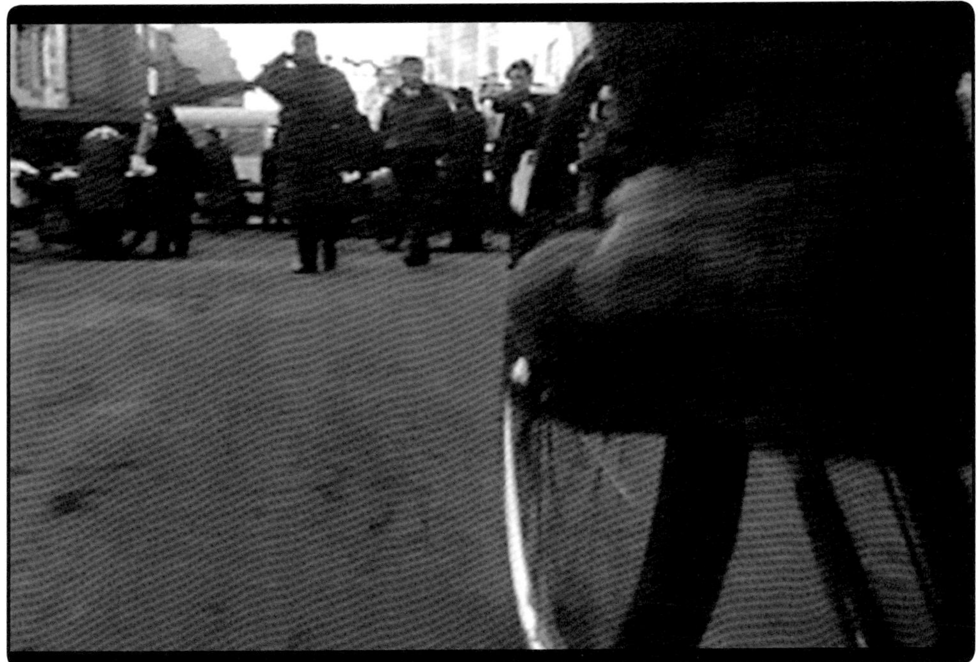

49   *The Day the Sun Turned Cold,* Bicycle

character of the tale like the first inch of a painted handscroll, which, according to the famous aphorism, reveals the essence of the whole picture. In *The Day the Sun Turned Cold* (Tianguo nizi; literally, *Heaven's Rebellious Son*), what turns cold is not the sun in the sky but a young man, a son—Guan Jian—the offspring of incompatible parentage between a strict Confucian (albeit Communist) father whom he fears and a warm, nurturing mother whom he loves (figs. 50–52). When Guan Jian turns up one day at the local police station to accuse his mother of having poisoned his father ten years

50   *The Day the Sun Turned Cold,*
The Oedipal Son

51   *The Day the Sun Turned Cold,*
The Stern Father

earlier, what—*really*—drives him on this relentless journey? What impels him on this quest for judgment? Why does he, so like his father, turn cold against his mother? What kind of "justice" could he be after? And how could any child of Chinese parents do something so shameful to his family's reputation? (*The Day the Sun Turned Cold* DVD, Scene 1).

When the police doubt the young man's story—after all, why did he wait ten years to tell it?—we are forced to focus more on the psychological question of personal motivation than on the detective's quest for the facts of the case. Guan Jian says he is doing it "for Dad," but we have also heard his dying father (Guan Shichang) whisper the injunction, "You're not a little boy anymore and there are things you ought to understand. You must keep them in your own heart and don't reveal them to any others. . . . No crying. . . . Don't cry"(fig. 53; *The Day the Sun Turned Cold* DVD, Scene 2). Why, then, when the father himself has clarified and reinforced the normative Chinese rules of response—emotional repression for the collective good rather than putting matters of private conscience out in public view—does young Guan Jian choose to "reveal" to all what he personally believes to be the shameful truth? What motivates him to elevate an individual conception of "justice" above loyalty to family? And is there even any truth to his accusation?

Perhaps deep down and unconsciously, Guan Jian longs to be—or is genetically disposed toward becoming—as stern and cold as his father, whether or not the facts of the case are there to back him up. "You talk just like your father," is his mother's response when he puts his accusation of murder directly to her. She utters this even before his words have come forth fully, as if to write the whole matter off to the psychodynamics of a conflicted parental relationship; but at the same time, in doing so, she implicitly acknowledges the depths of her troubled relationship with her husband and the Oedipal relation of the family triangle (*The Day the Sun Turned Cold* DVD, Scene 3). Both parents are locked in a battle for control—for the loyalty and

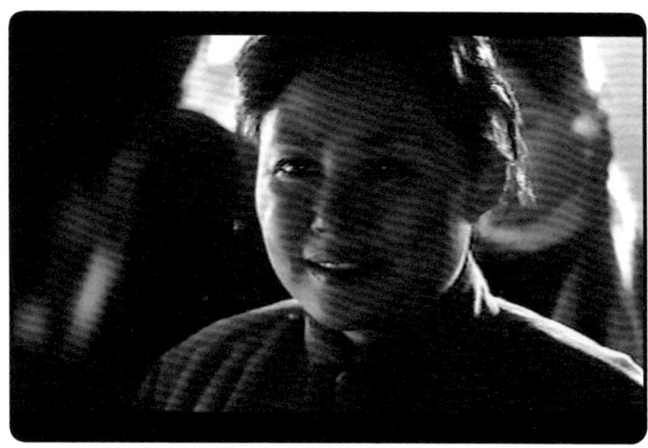

52   *The Day the Sun Turned Cold,* The Loving Mother

53   *The Day the Sun Turned Cold,* The Ambivalent Son

The Day the Sun Turned Cold, The Granary

soul—of the son, and for Guan Jian the attachment to mother runs just as deep as that to father. Steeped in the smoky optics of *film noir,* it is a film that knows its Hitchcock; and as in Hitchcock, optics wrap the film in a shroud of Freudian complexes. The steamy granary where the mother, Pu Fengying, boils up bean curd for the village market is recognizably authentic to anyone who has ever set foot in a smoke-filled Chinese peasant hut, but it is also coded for the steamy conflicts that are slowly brewing, while the perpetual haze is a reminder of the subjective filters through which the mysterious mother will be viewed throughout the film (fig. 54). As well as a gloomy nod to the *noir* world of cinematic corruption, crime, and personal anguish, all this smoke is a visual manifestation of the tormented soul that labors here—and worse, of the private hell that awaits her. Hot steam contrasts with the perpetual chill upon the land, which marks each puff of human breath and matches in temperature the increasing estrangement between family members, most striking when the wife and husband take turns standing out in the snow when the parental bed proves no less cold. As the angst-ridden mother, distinguished actress Siqin Gaowa herself exudes both heat and frost.

Like most of Hitchcock's heroes, our main character is obsessive in his maternal attachment: unmarried and highly vulnerable to Oedipal jealousies that surround him—in this case, charged not only by the hostile father but by a mother's rejection and the subversive intrusion of a romantic father-substitute. Based on a case study by

Zhang Chenggong of an actual crime that occurred in the People's Republic, but significantly altered by Yim Ho's screenplay,[1] the plot of this film turns on particulars; but beyond its particulars, what is signified by this typical family and its atypical tale? There is nothing unusual in China about a father-son conflict, and Chinese fiction abounds with such tales. That a son would openly rebel against a harsh father may not be so common, but it is nonetheless comprehensible. Ba Jin did so in real life, and he turned his rebellion into the classic modern novel *Family*.[2] And of course Mao Zedong did this in spades, rejecting the marriage his father arranged for him, then rejecting his father and ultimately taking this initial rebellion to great heights. But where do we find the Chinese precedent for a son to turn against a nurturing mother whom he truly loves? A model is hard to find, except symbolically in the great political rectification movements, when Maoist ideology turned family values on their head and Mao had himself placed at the head of all families, setting all family members against each other. Perhaps a political analog lurks behind this perverse tale, raising questions about public morality in China and delving into Hong Kong's peculiar relationship to its mainland parent (more will be discussed about this later). What concerns us most in this film is not some unusual crime, or the question of who-done-it, or even the lingering question of whether this "remembered" crime actually took place, but rather the unusual urge toward revelation and the reordering of the traditional Chinese canon that prioritizes family and shame to the detriment of self and guilt.

That the young man's thoughts should take such a turn puts his psychological health into question, and he knows it. The question is not just whether Guan Jian is correct or not, but whether he is sane or delusional. When first arriving at the police station, he has accidentally cut his hand—a wound that perhaps symbolizes the death of his father and his own fantasy role in this death as well as a prefigurement of the blood that will be let by his reporting this death as a murder. Shortly afterwards, as the captain is obliged to depart abruptly in the midst of their initial interview, the captain instructs the boy: "Kid, go to the hospital." Guan Jian replies, "I'm not crazy!" and in doing so sounds very much like a classic Hitchcock hero-victim. "Have your *hand* looked at," the captain is forced to explain, but only after the possibility has been laid out for continuing consideration that maybe, behind this restrained or restricted exterior, a very different kind of persona lurks inside (a shade of *Psycho*'s Norman Bates). Throughout the film, the officer serves not just as detective but also as the boy's psychiatrist (fig. 55). Moments before his reference to hospitalization, he had put his hand to Guan Jian's forehead to test whether the young man was feverish (DVD Scene 1: The Accusation). Much later on, in contrast to this, just when the audience is given evidence suggesting that Jian really *is* delusional, the captain comes to believe in him (in his sanity, his innocence, his accuracy), and pushes a stalled criminal investigation through to a conclusion, much like an analyst breaking down a patient's resistance by probing the hidden recesses of memory to recover a repressed dream. Only, this dream is a reality, and the truth of this matter when

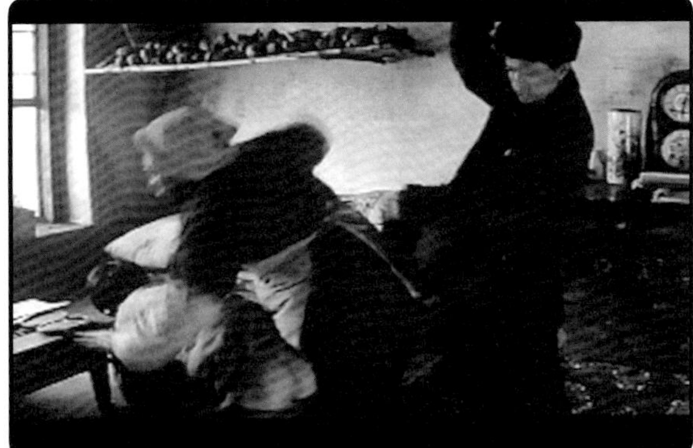

confirmed (like that fully exposed at the end of Hitchcock's *Vertigo*) becomes more devastating and more deadly than if it had remained fantasy.

When Guan Jian reveals to the police captain that he came to his conclusion about his father's death from reading a French crime case (and he displays a book on great criminal cases of the nineteenth and twentieth centuries in the West), the captain takes a dismissive turn toward Guan Jian ("Big fan of films and novels are you?" he asks, his anti-Western chauvinism clearly manifest). We are put on alert that the intrusion of Western thought is a precipitating element in Guan Jian's unorthodox behavior (DVD Scene 1: The Accusation). At more than one level the conflict here corresponds to differences between traditional Chinese and modern Western values and behaviors and indicates that the various borrowings in each of these three films—of Barbie-doll mermaids in *Suzhou River;* Dostoevskian doubles and Faulknerian time constructs in the film to come; *film noir* shadings in all three works—are more than just tropes or mere figurations about Westernization. Rather, they are part of an ever-deepening process of assimilation and globalization in Chinese culture and Chinese-language film culture. The close examination in *The Day the Sun Turned Cold* of Chinese and Western normative psychology as a cinematic theme is an event-horizon in Chinese-language filmmaking.

If a Chinese filmmaker hopes to embrace Alfred Hitchcock, he must also give Professor Freud a hug, and Hong Kong director Yim Ho does just that. "The relation of a boy to his father is, as we say, an 'ambivalent' one," claims the doctor,[3] and Guan Jian is indeed a very ambivalent son. On the one hand, the father is a schoolmaster, and the son is a truant. Guan Jian lies to the father about his absences from school and cheats on his homework, for which his father beats him mercilessly ("I'll kill you, you little scumbag. . . . I'll beat him to an inch of his life") and finally exclaims, "Guan Jian, you're no son of mine" (fig. 56). The mother offers an alternate experience, shielding the boy from his father's blows and nurturing him warmly, which in turn earns the father's epithet (in the boy's presence) that she is "spoiling him rotten" and that "he will grow up to be a beancurd seller like you." The father's measure of virtue in relation to his son is his own reputation: "I Guan Shichang am a model teacher. . . . a paragon of virtue. And you dare bring disgrace on my name!" On the other hand, still eager to win his father's love by alternate means, when Guan Jian discovers his mother cheating on his father and denying it, he reports her deception and undoubtedly enjoys the degree of bonding with his father that this earns (fig. 53; *The Day the Sun Turned Cold* DVD, Scene 2). This "classic" pattern is reminiscent of Cao Xueqin's *Dream of the Red Chamber*, in which Jia Shen beats the book's hero, Baoyu, mercilessly, raging that "Merely by fathering a monster like this I have proved myself an unfilial son [and] now that I have the opportunity at last, I may as well finish off what I have begun and put him down, like the vermin he is, . . ."[4] only to be thwarted in his "filial" revenge by his mother and wife. In the traditional "stern father, compassionate mother" world, the operant principle is that "the mother is close but not respected, while the father has respect but not closeness."[5]

Margery Wolf offers an anthropological account by which Guan Jian's distant relationship with his father and his intimate relationship with his mother are perfectly normal by traditional standards. After the age of six or seven, she writes,

> social pressure and the father's own understanding of "what is right" force him to create a social distance between himself and his son. . . . fathers say that it is only from this aloof distance that they can engender in their sons the proper behavior of a good adult. "You cannot be your son's friend and correct his behavior." A child will not take seriously the friendly suggestions of an obviously loving adult, but he will obey the commands of a stern, feared parent. This philosophy, of course, reflects (or is reflected in) the educational techniques of Chinese schools even today. . . . A Chinese father wants respect and obedience even at the price of fear or dislike. . . . He is aided in his endeavors by the sanctions of his culture, the example of his neighbors, and the teachings of the schools.[6]

Nevertheless, Wolf concludes, "As young men sons may fear their fathers, but they nonetheless emulate them, rejecting the open intimacy desired by their mothers in favor of a more manly stance."[7] A Chinese mother, on the other hand

> would certainly appreciate her son's respect and obedience, but not at the price of his affection. Her marriage into a family of strangers has forced her to depend entirely on herself in constructing working relationships. . . . Chinese culture extracts from a son the obligation of supporting his mother and showing her a minimum degree of respect; but a woman's experience with

social sanctions has usually been that they have operated against her position rather than in any way promoting it. Far more dependable are the ties of affection and gratitude that she weaves in the years of her son's childhood. . . . Chinese society has given a father both the power and the authority to manage his adult sons. A mother's authority is not so clearly stated, and so she must establish her power in a more subtle fashion. For her, the father's method of withdrawal into formality would be both difficult and dangerous.[8]

Incomplete in this persuasive account of family norms are the attendant psychodynamics, the carefully observed inner life of jealousy and desire, fear and frustration, guilt and transference, by which Yim Ho's film marks Guan Jian as abnormal by Chinese standards but renders these abnormalities psychologically comprehensible to the viewer.[9]

The normative relationship of sons too closely attached to mothers has bred in China a male culture (particularly among the wealthy scholar class) that in a relative sense may be seen as "favoring femininity over masculinity."[10] Eugene Wang, quoted in the previous chapter, suggests that "As the aspired-to stillness and passivity [of Chinese filial culture] have touches of femininity, femininity itself becomes a condition highly aspired to. Instead of being afflicted by castration anxiety, the problematic of the lack is quite reversed in the Chinese cultural context. It is the man who lacks. If anything, a femininity complex would be the appropriate form of the unconscious in the Chinese psyche."[11] In *The Day the Sun Turned Cold*, with the parents at odds with each other (theirs was an arranged marriage, which the mother sought to escape in their first year together) and frequently at odds over their son, Guan Jian is well positioned to play his parents off against one another with a gaming strategy that doesn't allow for the attainment of any resolution between their conflicted hatreds and his conflicted attachment to each of them but that ultimately extends to him an Hitchcockian awareness of their expendability. As with *Dream of the Red Chamber*'s Baoyu, there is a passive personality—here turned passive-aggressive, strong suggestions of homosexuality, and enormous psychic conflict over which of the warring parents to please and identify with.

In a Freudian view there is no doubt a bit of the parricide in the boy's fantasy life, and perhaps even a good deal more than that since he can scarcely hope to please them both or even preserve a good relationship with both parents.[12] He can seek his father's favor by becoming more like him, a severe, proud, intellectual disciplinarian, but only at the expense of losing his mother's affection. By the age of twenty-four, Guan Jian is intellectually rigorous and forthright but emotionally reserved, absolutely proper and bound up in high principle, very much like Dad. And indeed, when he later demands that his mother account for Guan Shichang's death (even begs to forgive her, if she would only bond with him in the intense intimacy of sharing of her secret guilt), her dismissive response is to *accuse him* of sounding just

57 *The Day the Sun Turned Cold,*
The Confrontation

58 *The Day the Sun Turned Cold,*
Police Captain

like his father (fig. 57). It can no doubt be imagined that he might choose to maximize his relationship with his mother, seeking to escape his father's wrath and secure his mother's affection for himself alone As a fourteen-year-old progressing from latency into adolescence, he is becoming aware of the sexual life. He has long had visual access to the parental bed, and now through flashback—his eyes and subjective memory—the police captain and the film audience are shown the father's sexual overtures rejected by the mother. As his father leaves the now-sterile marital bed for the cold of night, heading out of doors to cool his anger, cannot Guan Jian imagine himself filling the void? It is a moment that poses psychological alternatives for the longer term, as long as the mother remains at the center of Guan Jian's sexual universe. Should she not be ready for him, he can delay his own sexual life, remaining single (as he does), celibate, and ascetic in order to remain ever available. ("I don't go to movies, or listen to music, or read novels. I don't even watch TV." He also "doesn't smoke, drink, gamble, or play around with women.") Or he might even become homosexual so that his sexual activities do not tarnish his idealized image of her. There is some hint of this possibility in the film, both in his manner and particularly in the ingratiating relationship he quickly develops with the hard-boiled, Bogartlike police captain investigating the case (fig. 58).

In the classic Freudian world, the parricidal fantasy is universal and central to psychological development. Out of *it,* the analyst tells us, comes the sense of guilt. And out of an unhealthy adjustment to the conditions that give rise to it grow narcissism, masochism, and sadism.[13] In a Freudian world, it is only natural that if the harshly punished son's deep-seated fantasies of his father's death should turn into reality that this would give rise to the fear that he was himself somehow responsible, exaggerating the development of guilt feelings with which he must come to grips. Uncertain of the real cause of his father's death but fixated on the matter, Guan Jian becomes a student of Western crime stories and eventually comes to attend night school in criminal law, through which he discovers examples that develop an alternate fantasy, that his mother (whom he once vaguely saw putting "something" in the father's food) was actually a poisoner (though she says this was just MSG). Being used to leveraged negotiations for affection with his antagonistic parents, he is now in a position to negotiate for higher stakes: he can favor his mother, accept his own imagined guilt for his father's death, and, by absolving his mother of any public suspicion, can serve as both her liberator and secure her affections. Or he can identify with his father, imagine the guilt as hers (doing this "for Dad," as he puts it), sacrifice Mom in order to absolve the guilt of his own patricidal fantasies, and win his father's long-sought love, posthumous but eternal.

Wherever this detective tale leads, whatever the forensic truth of exhumations and laboratory analyses reveals, the psychodrama of Yim Ho's film has a life and depth of its own. What complicates this Oedipal triangle is its intersection with a second triangle. When Guan Shichang is replaced in Pu Fengying's affections, and then in her bed, it is not by the son but by an intruder, an outsider who has perhaps "earned" this right by having saved the lives of both the mother and the son. The intruder is a young woodsman, Liu Dagui. Unlike the stern and bookish father, Liu is lively and humorous (fig. 59). The father is an educator-bureaucrat, a mouthpiece in society for the powers that be: Confucianist or Maoist, he's utilitarian through and through. When Guan Jian asks the woodsman why loggers cry out "Timber," the father intervenes to say that it's to warn others not to get hurt. "Trees are only useful if you chop them down," he explains. But the woodcutter is rural, uneducated (like the

59 *The Day the Sun Turned Cold,* Liu Dagui

mother), probably a Manchu, and a man of nature. For him (and as we shall see in *Good Men, Good Women*), the tree is a living thing, and "'Timber' [is] how we say farewell to the spirit of the tree." He also awakens the spirit in Pu Fengying. Despite his father's repudiations of him, Guan Jian longs to be his father's beloved son, and when Liu comes between his father and Pu Fengying, Guan shifts his fidelity toward the father. He peers in on the lovers' infidelity (disclosed visually by a symbolic flow of seeds in the family grain mill) and reports it to Guan Shichang, thus playing a critical role in the sequence of events that leads to his father's death. This justifies a sense of responsibility for the event that either has to be absorbed as guilt or transferred to the mother as blame. That such a targeting of the mother can take place is first revealed to the young boy by a beating he witnesses his father giving to Pu Fengying for her dalliance with Liu Dagui. This allows Guan Jian to observe parental punishment extended beyond the authoritarian father-son relationship, revealing to him the sadistic fantasy (and libidinal pleasure) of punishing Pu Fengying himself for her collateral guilt in turning not to him from the father, but to the alternate, illicit lover.[14] And it marks the beginning of a deeper identification with Guan Shichang, father-as-avenger, as a mechanism for negotiating his own Oedipal frustrations.

That punishment of the mother by the husband is both socially normative and perhaps even subtly pleasurable for her as well (or should be, if she has come to publicly embrace the social norms) is suggested by one of the old female villagers visiting the ailing Guan Shichang, and she even tosses in a little imagined mayhem to spice up her smiling remarks: "The old girl [Pu Fengying] needs a good beating. When I was first married, my husband beat me too. Broke lots of brooms over my back. I wanted to murder him. But look, I got through it" (*The Day the Sun Turned Cold* DVD, Scene 2). Freud would suggest that it is only natural for Guan Jian to fantasize both killing his father and playing husband to his mother. In actually playing the role of informant on his mother and thus (however indirectly) taking on the role of his mother's executioner as well, Guan Jian does more than just fantasize. It is through this that he comes closest to taking on the husband's role.

Just as the film's opening image captures the fateful dynamic of the plot with a bicycle negotiating an urban setting, its wheels going round and round like justice, setting forth with a fateful mechanicity (a modern and Western device, somewhat like the hybrid boy who sets it in motion), so too a series of subsequent images establish a rural parallel. Bicycle wheels and pedals are transmuted into a grindstone traveling a closed circle in the rural family granary (traditional, like the family Guan Jian left behind), a mill wheel whose wordless recurrence throughout the remainder of the film serves as a narrative marker as justice runs its course. The first time it is seen, when all is still more or less well in the household, the wheel is driven by the family donkey, led by the sister. The family works in harmony except for Guan Shichang, who moments later arrives on the scene to break the initial nostalgic spell and deliver Guan Jian a stiff beating (fig. 60). Seen a second time, the donkey is still driving the mill

<table>
<tr><td>60</td><td>The Day the Sun Turned Cold, The Mill Wheel</td><td>61</td><td>The Day the Sun Turned Cold, "Who'd Marry Me?"</td></tr>
</table>

wheel but has been abandoned by the alienated mother during an illicit tryst in the grain-storage loft above; this is spied upon but not wholly understood by young Guan Jian. The mill wheel is put into service a third time for a family feast when Jian returns home as a young adult, initiated as a reconciliation but concluding as a fruitless interrogation of the mother by the son about his father's death. Pu Fengying here takes the place of the donkey, laboring for her son's love but straining the Oedipal relationship by her refusal to confess her crime to him or, thereby, to make him the dominant male in her life. In a fourth and final view, Jian returns home for a last time, temporarily obliged by forensic evidence to believe in his mother's innocence and intending fully to reconcile with her. Emasculated, in effect, and submissive, he falls to his knees calling himself "a bastard," as if to reaffirm her parenthood while denying his father's. This time, Guan Jian symbolically takes his mother's place at the mill wheel, but the mill is no longer productive. The damage is done, and as he gives the wheel one last turn, the plot moves toward its tragic conclusion, reversing the relationship of the moment and leading to her conviction.

All of this provides an elegantly structured if not entirely original situation. Psychoanalytically, much of it reads like a Chinese Hamlet, fitting the classic Western schema with a murderous stepfather, a hero's lengthy irresolution, and, as a denouement, the hero's avenging the father's death not only for the mother's complicity in crime but equally for her rejection of him in favor of a "third man."[15] Guan's sister, Guan Qing, in the absence of a female companion, plays the Ophelia of the lot in terms of being the collateral victim; she laments, "Which of you have ever thought of me? When Ma remarried, people spat on me. Now you're back stirring things up and Ma's reputation is smeared . . . who'd marry me, her daughter? Jian, has this ever occurred to you?" (fig. 61). Guan Jian's "resolution" of the situation, like Hamlet's, requires the destruction not just of Guan Qing/Ophelia but of the entire family unit. Read culturally, dramatic circumstances polarize the alternatives and leave Guan Jian unable to escape a choice between psychological fulfillment or social sanction, guilt versus shame. He reverses the Chinese father's injunction not to "reveal" these matters but to "keep them in your own heart," to swallow his guilt and spare the family shame, and follows instead the urging of Hamlet's father's ghost to "revenge his foul and most unnatural murder."[16] But he is also driven to surpass the parental ghost's urging of restraint, for Hamlet to avenge the illicit lover but leave the mother's punishment to the inner experience of her own guilt and to Heaven's retribution: "Against thy mother aught. Leave her to Heaven / And to those thorns that in her bosom lodge / To prick and sting her."[17] And he takes his mother, not her lover, as the primary target of his vengeance. Although Guan Jian claims to act in the name of the father, Yim Ho's remarkable analysis reveals the emotional conflicts, the motivation, and the ambivalence that bond the child to his parents, not merely in terms of traditional filial obligation *(xiao)* but also in terms of the psychodynamic forces undergirding male identity formation. More than attaining social justice, gaining his mother's submission and becoming the "Oedipal victor" in his parental conflicts lurk at the heart of the matter. On visiting his mother on her last day in jail, Guan Jian tells her, in terms that reflect more on himself than on her: "Ma, you've brought this on yourself. That day by the grindstone, I asked you, 'Yes or no.' Why didn't you just nod? If you'd just told me, things wouldn't have ended up like this."

Freud wrote that "It can scarcely be owing to chance that three of the masterpieces of the literature of all time—the *Oedipus Rex* of Sophocles, Shakespeare's *Hamlet* and Dostoevsky's *The Brothers Karamazov*—should all deal with the same subject: parricide. In all three, moreover, the motive for the deed, sexual rivalry for a woman, is laid bare."[18] There is certainly much of Hamlet in the triangular affair of the adults and the conflicted feelings toward each parent that leads Guan Jian to delay at length before striking out at his mother in the symbolic name of his father and the normative rule of law that his father stands for. Regarding the uncertainty and delayed exposure with which Shakespearean literature delivers its criminal justice and psychological resolution, Freud put it well: "Poetic treatment," he wrote, "is impossible without softening and disguise."[19] "Disguise" for Guan Jian means that only by blaming the mother can he relieve himself of whatever guilt he feels both for the hatred of his father and the longing for his mother. "Conscience *(liangxin)*," he tells his mother, is what motivated him. But in doing so, he can also identify *in guilt* with the mother, fusing these sources of guilt with the further guilt he accrues by betraying his mother, all the while identifying *through vengeance* with his father. Thus, a resolution of sorts can finally be effected in the filial psyche for his estrangement from his mutually estranged parents and the ambivalence of his Oedipal conflicts. As a by-product, he can also assure the separation of his mother from his acquired rival, Liu Dagui.

The Day the Sun Turned Cold is not alone among the three films studied here in its Oedipal structure. *Suzhou River,* too, offers a striking series of triangulated relationships that deserve recounting, beginning with Mudan's being spurned by her father and thrust on the stranger Mada so that the father can carry on with his prostitutes (fig. 3). When Mada becomes an infatuation for Mudan, this is in part as a father substitute. She stumbles into an unstable and ultimately deadly relationship with Mada and his gangster girlfriend, Xiao Hong. Seen through a psychoanalytic lens, Mada's relationship with Xiao Hong is easily broken because of Mada's inability to enter into romantic commitment (a Freudian/Oedipal/Hitchcockian standard), and Xiao Hong uses this very same weakness to enlist his participation and gain her revenge on the young and defenseless Mudan. So when Mada forsakes Mudan for a mere forty thousand yuan, and her wealthy father, too, has played her cheap in the kidnap bargain, her betrayal comes from the hands of both men at once (fig. 2). When Mada seeks to reconstruct the relationship, he stumbles into a different triangle, and in the second part of the film's dynamic, he comes between Meimei (his substitute for Mudan) and her videographer lover. Mada is a singleton—watching videos, perhaps pornographic, all night long is his substitute for a relationship—and probably a mother's boy, like so many Hitchcock figures. Having proved unable to love the real (available) Mudan, perhaps because of Mom (though we can only guess at this), he now dedicates himself to the pursuit of an ideal; he forgets her childish machinations to focus only on her imagined purity with the effect of breaking up the *real* relationship of the narcissistic Meimei and the film's voyeuristic narrator. And since it is his pursuit of an abstraction that defines his own virtue, once his pursuit has led him back to the real Mudan, their mutual demise seems inevitable, an irony of mythic proportions that belatedly costs him his life in return for the death he subjected Mudan to long ago. At this point, with her own triangular relationship with Mada and the nameless videographer shattered, Meimei undergoes a transformation that structures the third and final dynamic of the film (or post-film), rejecting the videographer in order to triangulate herself with the deceased Mada and Mudan and the ideal they have come to represent.

On reflection, then, Oedipal forces play a structural role throughout *Suzhou River,* and guilt provides an underlying force. But only in *The Day the Sun Turned Cold* is the very nature of this guilt subjected to scrupulous interrogation and its deeper cultural implications examined. *Suzhou River,* which is rich in Freudian triples, at its core is based on a series of Hitchcock-like (and ultimately, Dostoevskian) doubles. The reverse is true of *The Day the Sun Turned Cold.* The doubles derive their primary meaning from the Oedipal triangle they construct: Guan Jian's uncertain identification with each parent derives from the intense, mutual, and irreconcilable hostility between them. Had Pu Fengying not murdered Guan Shichang, we can only wonder what Guan Jian might have done himself. Given that she did, this leaves only his mother to kill, which in a sense he does in a failed effort to take his father's place.

And when he does this, since he has never really externalized his mother, he is also punishing and killing himself.

Regardless of the cultural globalization evident in all three of these films, each of their borrowings must be considered in a local cultural context to understand not only what is borrowed but *how* it has been borrowed and applied. Western viewers may be struck that what is most evident here are classic Freudian principles. One might derive them from American film (citing Hitchcock here as a convenience requires a reference to England as well) more than any of the divergent post-Freudian modes. That this could be dismissed as marginally *retarditaire*, just as China's "avant-garde" art of the past two decades sometimes has been, matters little to Chinese-language audiences. What matters is whether it serves the local purpose, and here—with a kind of reverse Orientalism, holding up an external mirror in order to reflect internal criticism—it serves that purpose well. Traditional Chinese family values posit a set of behavioral ideals that are virtually the opposite of those considered normative by Freudian standards: above all, lifelong fidelity and submission to parents (*xiao*) outranks and often preempts the pursuit of romantic choice and the development of spousal affection.

> (A son) should not forget his parents in a single lifting up of his feet, and therefore he will walk in the highway and not take a by-path, he will use a boat and not attempt to wade through a stream;—not daring, with the body left him by his parents, to go in the way of peril. He should not forget his parents in the utterance of a single word, and therefore an evil word will not issue from his mouth, and an angry word will not come back to his person. Not to disgrace his person and not to cause shame to his parents may be called filial duty [*xiao*].[20]

But it is not my point here to define an adequate local substitute for classical Freudianism that would better serve as a Chinese model: "China" itself is much too diverse and too highly contested an entity for that.[21] Rather, imported Freudian concepts have been brought to bear in this film as a counterweight to traditional Chinese values and assumptions. *This* Freudianism, like Dr. Freud's well-known cigar,[22] is laden with alternate value and takes on shades of meaning in the critique of things Chinese that it might never have elsewhere.

In all cultures, external and internalized sources of moral motivation are bound to overlap, and the distinction in adults is bound to be imprecise; developmental psychologists and cultural anthropologists may dispute which to emphasize. But open almost any traditional Chinese text, whether philosophical or fictional, and an emphasis on external display will be apparent. The Ming-dynasty short story "Magistrate Teng Settles the Case of Inheritance with Ghostly Cleverness" provides an elegant example:

All of the classics and scriptures of the three teachings of our time serve the same purpose of exhorting people to virtue. Confucianism has the Thirteen Classics, the Six Classics, and the five Classics; Buddhism has the many volumes of the *Tripitaka;* and Daoism has the *Zhuangzi,* the *Liezi,* and so forth. However, all of these volumes that fill up trunks and clutter desks are in fact quite superfluous, for, as I see it, only two words suffice to make a good person: *xiao* and *di*—filial piety and fraternal love. Again, of these two, just *xiao,* "filial piety," would suffice. Those who show filial piety to their parents and love and honor whatever their parents love and honor will, for the sake of the parents, extend such feelings to their brothers, who are like branches on the same tree. Thus, how can there be any lack of harmony?[23]

Emphasis here should be placed on the words "whatever" and "for the sake of the parents." This Chinese reading of Chinese standards—the prefatory remarks are fulfilled in the short story about sibling rivalry that follows—is that social obligation to the family, and particularly to the senior member of the family, takes priority over internal responsivity to any individually perceived sense of right and wrong; that the delayed transfer of moral leadership until the passing of one's elders minimizes conflict between the generations; and that the broad application of these principles beyond the family operates best for the maintenance of social harmony both within and beyond the family. The effect of this, by contemporary Western standards, is that whatever their chronological age, sons and daughters remain as moral children throughout the life of their parents (and parents-in-law, in the case of daughters), continuing to internalize standards of right and wrong into their adult years by forever basing individual conscience on the moral instruction of their elders; and more broadly, that by this, obligations within the local family unit (which remains the primary source of standards for moral behavior) are given priority over ethical obligations to the larger public sphere. This essential Chinese model emphasizes harmony and stability and aims toward a perception that fundamental ideals have long been in place that have not and cannot be improved upon (despite the reality of ongoing changes in Chinese moral philosophy and jurisprudence throughout the centuries). The essential contemporary perceptual Western model instead dispatches stability in favor of an endless quest to refine the definitions of moral standards and a continuing struggle toward their private and public application to constantly changing times and circumstances.

As for the intersection of this timeless model with temporal practicalities and the convergence of morality with psychology, Beijing-born author Jianying (Jane) Zha, in her compelling *China Pop: How Soap Operas, Tabloids, and Bestsellers Are Transforming a Culture,* writes,

This is a country where nobody confesses sins. Massive destructions have occurred, atrocities have been committed, millions have died of starvation and

persecution . . . husbands have denounced wives, people have sold friend-
ships for a casual nod from a Party secretary—yet it has *never* been popular to
acknowledge openly the wrongs you have done to others. . . . the question about
the collective Chinese memory lingers and gnaws. . . . In fact it's hard to talk
about psychological issues in Chinese—the language just isn't well equipped
with words and expressions to discuss your inner demons. The common attitude is to leave the demons alone. Let bygones be bygones. Let's look ahead. . . .
There are too many skeletons in everyone's closet; once you started opening
one, there's no telling where things would end.[24]

In short, the fear of public shame stands in the way of acknowledging private guilt.
And so, in a cultural context, where personal denial and collective cultural amnesia
overwrite historical memory and are given historical moral sanction, what tale could
be more revealing of China's ethical constraints and taboos than *The Day the Sun
Turned Cold*, where automatic disbelief that so unfilial an accusation could ever be
made gradually gives way to an examination of the cold, hard facts of the case? No
crime is even suspected when the son accuses his mother of crime. And yet, as the son
presents *his* perceptions through flashbacks (often accompanied by Japanese avant-
garde composer Otomo Yoshihide's poignant Schubertian, cello-driven chamber
music), his visual narration forces his imagination not only on a cinematic casting of
dubious policemen and astonished neighbors but on the *real* viewing audience, on an
unprepared society at large. He is not exactly confessing to his own crime, individually committed, but to one by which the entire family is shamed. His accusation therefore comes as a form of group confession: look what *my family* has done! Even the
father, Guan Shichang, bears part of the blame for his own demise. Ironically, as a
collective matter, such guilt falls within the domain of family dynamics rather than
being an isolated, individual measure, thus locating common moral ground for the
Chinese experience and the European psychodynamic model.[25]

Among Chinese-language films, *The Day the Sun Turned Cold* by analogy makes,
or at least allows for, a most unusual statement; I know of no other quite like it. In a
culture that historically places family ahead of nation and shame ahead of guilt, if a
mother can be denounced by her own loving son, then surely the Chinese nation and
its culture are subject to denunciation by its own people and maybe even to a little
rebellion. The original Chinese title, *Tianguo nizi* (Heaven's Rebellious Son), seems
to give its blessing to this Freudian rebel. But there exists yet another level, a symbolic analog, to this group confession.

Freud understood well the extension from home to state of attitudes toward authority, referring repeatedly in Dostoevsky's case to "the Little Father, the Tsar."[26] Projected
from the Chinese family model, to which Freudian psychology is here attached as a
critical apparatus, is a political analog, ancient and well known to all. This family-to-
state equation, distinctive when it was formulated in Confucius' time, became a model

for all later times: the emperor as the Big Father. Confucius urged the governors he advised to behave with the same responsibility that adults have toward their children so that they might earn from their subjects the respect that good children naturally offer to good parents. For Freud, it is precisely this symbolic inscription of paternal powers, of the father writ large, which describes the tensions and lights the universal desire toward patricide:

> A son's picture of his father is habitually clothed with excessive powers of this kind, and it is found that distrust of the father is intimately linked with admiration for him. . . . The taboo does not only pick out the king and exalt him above all common mortals, it also makes his existence a torment and an intolerable burden.[27]

It is here where Lacan enters with his "Name-of-the-father," which "sustains the structure of desire with the structure of the law,"[28] and it is here where we must realize that the force of *The Day the Sun Turned Cold* could scarcely be sustained without this symbolic dimension. In the past century, transcending all intentions to sanctify or dethrone Confucius' teachings, with the rise of a self-conscious nation-building effort, the inscription of Chinese polity in terms of family dynamics has received considerable ideological reinforcement, retooling, and refinement.[29]

Tani Barlow writes that in the Communist era,

> The modern socialist *jiating* [family] and the Maoist *guojia* [state] coexisted in unity—as concept metaphors of each other. This is how I interpret mobilizations like the 1957 campaign "Industrious and Frugal in Establishing the Nation, Industrious and Frugal in Managing the Family," where state and family are virtually synonymous; what operated in one sphere translates directly into the other. . . . The work of housewives (*jiating zhufu*) must exactly mirror the work going on outside the *jiating* in the *guojia*. The same is true of *guojia* (post-monarchy nation/state), which partakes of an older social formation, *guo* (empire), and *jiating*, meaning a contemporary domestic unit that formed in part as a reaction to *jia* (patriline).[30]

Expanding on this equation, in the gendered world of Chinese culture it has long been commonplace for people to think of the government (whether emperor or Communist Party, the authoritarian half of the public-private equation) in patriarchal terms; here is the ultimate Father. In the third century B.C.E., the statesman-poet Qu Yuan—today regarded as China's *national* poet—quested after recognition from his ruler, *male* of course, by parading himself in verse as the ruler's would-be *bride*.[31] China itself (the land, its culture, its people) is referred to maternally; this is the Motherland. The royal Father, ruling over this Motherland, is typically remote, conceived of as

Other: "Heaven is high, the emperor far away," as the famous expression goes (*tian gao, di yuan*); and something of the same goes for every household father. Even for the male child, it is the mother with whom one will ordinarily feel most intimate and the father from whom he will (may, must) feel estranged. The child-self is the extension of the mother. In stunning contrast to the many dissenting (if not outright dissident) films about events in the People's Republic that have played primarily to international audiences since 1985, the alleged crime explored by *The Day the Sun Turned Cold* is not ascribed to the father, the Party, the Other, but rather to the mother, the self. It is, most unusually, a crime *against* the father/the State; and at another level, a level that can never be resolved in terms of *legal* justice and only managed in terms of psychological comprehension, a crime to which the entire family, including the overbearing father himself, is complicit.

What I suspect is involved in the political formulation of this film is the people finally taking responsibility for China's collective misbehavior (criminality) rather than ascribing all this to the Communist Party or transferring it onto a tiny clique within the Party and forever playing the role of hapless victim to China's patriarchal authority. As a parable of China, it deals with opening that long-closed closet door that Jane Zha was talking about. It forces us to consider, in complex terms, what would happen if China, with its load of unacknowledged guilt, began to operate socially and psychologically more like a Western culture. It seems even to suggest that one of the prerequisites for China's becoming "modern" is developing the ability to experience and publicly express guilt, even at the expense of enduring shame. In the collective sense, that involves new modes of acknowledging and learning from history, of learning from and absorbing other cultures. The staged conflict here between Western and traditional norms is given a backhanded presentation, quoted previously, by one of the village women who shows up to support Principal Guan in his illness:

> The old girl [Pu Fengying] needs a good beating. When I was first married, my husband beat me too. Broke lots of brooms over my back. I wanted to murder him. But look, I got through it. All of us went through that. What's this *Western* garbage about divorce? Doesn't she care about face?

On the other hand, this film suggests that the Chinese family (the polity, the culture) might well be torn apart by such "modernization," by so radical an ethical transformation, leaving as much structural damage and as few traces of warmth and attachment as one finds in the Guan-Pu family by the end of the film. Beyond all the other expressions of emotional torture in *The Day the Sun Turned Cold,* witness the sweater knit by Pu Fengying in prison, in her last days, as her last offering of warmth and nurture to an increasingly coldhearted and unforgiving son. There is a powerful symbol of contested control here: the sweater is decorated with the image of the horse, the year of Guan Jian's birth, translating the "offering" into the threat of Pu Fengying's

The Day the Sun Turned Cold, The Prison

The Day the Sun Turned Cold, Carted Away

indestructible maternal authority over him. Resistant, Guan Jian asks her to give it to his sister Qing instead. A few moments later, losing the cool, calculated, and emotionally aloof resolve that has possessed him throughout most of the film, he races from the jail with the sweater in hand, then dashes it into the back of a passing peasant's cart (figs. 62 and 63). The film then closes by juxtaposing this passing image with a remembered view of Liu Dagui's cart, a vehicle of rescue but ultimately of family doom (fig. 64). The various dualities of this conclusion are unresolved: the conclusion represents a departure, an undefining; where Guan Jian is now running to remains entirely uncertain; definition remains elusive, for while he has won in the name of the father, his "success" is a tragic failure. This conclusion-by-departure is shared with both *Suzhou River* (Meimei's disappearance, visualized only by a note that reads *"lai zhao wo ba,"* "Come and find me!") and *Good Men, Good Women* (as will be seen, in Chiang Bi-Yu's death coupled with Liang Ching's departure to Guangzhou), but in both of those films undefinition and absence come about through the pursuit of a remaining if somewhat slim measure of hope and not the kind of unanticipated and desperate uncertainty that grips Guan Jian in the end.

Finally, as a Hong Kong film (a fact that might be easily overlooked by a Western audience while watching this mainland story in a mainland setting) made in anticipation of the colony's historic handover to the People's Republic, it is scarcely possible until after the film's conclusion to contemplate its deeply lodged commentary on Hong Kong's relationship to China. Yim Ho has repeatedly visited this cinematic territory.[32] *The Day the Sun Turned Cold* seems to operate in a different realm from the cops-and-robbers and martial arts films that for the outside world have come to represent Hong Kong's film industry as a whole; for students of Hong Kong film, such films embody the colony's rebellious energy, its refusal to respect the limitations imposed by external powers, and its generalized distrust of authority.[33] By seeming to abandon Hong Kong itself for an authentic tale set in north China (fig. 64), Yim Ho leaves behind the dense population, the impersonal apartments, the contradictions of striking wealth and scarce resources, and the avoidance of emotional engagement that characterize

64 *The Day the Sun Turned Cold,* Snow Country/Liu's Cart

the island's urban lifestyle and play so well in Hong Kong "art-house films" such as Wong Kar-Wai's *Chungking Express* (1994) and *Fallen Angels* (1995).[34] Filmed in China with a Chinese cast, the very absence of a visible Hong Kong suggests the usurpation of the place and culture by the larger Chinese mainland domain. But however different their means, many of these films share similar core concerns.

While post-revolution Hong Kong came to be modeled on old Shanghai and in turn served as a model for Shanghai's economic and political rebirth under Jiang Zemin, Hong Kong's fears at the time of the changing of the guard from British bobbies to agents of the Public Security Bureau were vested primarily in the impending reimposition of mainland China's old-fashioned, rural-minded authoritarianism. The question that lingers is whether its future direction consists primarily of being driven backwards in time, into the arms of its old Father. In *The Day the Sun Turned Cold*, it is Guan Shichang who embodies the scarcely changing image of Chinese paternal authority. He is both the stern teacher of Confucian pieties and the strict enforcer of Communist education. Authoritarian, yet neither physically strong nor even very masculine, he is merely stern and vengeful—a representative of the older ruling generation, cuckolded by a younger man for all the neighbors to see yet supported by the community. While imposing a symbolic equation would be to critique the wife too narrowly, Pu Fengying is in many ways an effective trope for Mother Britannia. (Is it mere coincidence that even the "ying" in her name is shared with "Yingguo"—England?)[35] She is regal in bearing yet dowdy, warmly nurturing yet secretive, crafty in the protection of her authority, maternally devoted but in the end unfaithful. Like England, her authority is transgressive and extralegal: having expropriated Hong Kong in order to force the "poison" of opium (*du*) down China's throat, she is a murderous wife. And Guan Jian, alert to the shortcomings of both parents, unable to quite attach to either and yet quite unable to let go of either, what could he be if not the alienated soul of Hong Kong, a small figure pinned between two giants? Like Hong Kong, Guan Jian is resourceful, efficient, and able despite his diminutive status to manipulate the balance of power between the parental forces. Yet ultimately, because of the massive disparity in status, he is unable to convert this impact into any form of independence for himself or establish an identity apart from his continuing struggle against superior forces. Like Guan Jian, Hong Kong is limited to playing the colonizing forces off against one another and, in the end, given the transgressions of the mother, it has little alternative to reconciliation with the superior authority of the father.

In this family allegory, *The Day the Sun Turned Cold* identifies Hong Kong's Chinese parentage as a not wholly desirable yet inescapable part of its cultural experience. It conforms with Stephen Teo's assertion regarding the "eagerness of Hong Kong film-makers to delve into the past," to the effect that

> there is a genuine attempt to explore history and to acknowledge, even if only grudgingly, Hong Kong's kinship with China's history, both in its glorious and tragic manifestations, while at the same time inscribing a wish to stick one's head in the sand and to efface the history that looms on the horizon by effacing the 'real' history of the past. The eclecticism that underpins Hong Kong's type of postmodernism can thus be seen as a sign of a culture caught in the tension between a desire to construct a non-colonial identity by mobilising a sense of the past, and a profound anxiety about the possibility of that very identity being imposed rather than being constructed autonomously.[36]

It further submits that even if Hong Kong doesn't bear responsibility for everything that has been packed historically into China's massive closet of skeletons, Hong Kong and the People's Republic nonetheless share the same cultural closet, and what happens once that closet door is opened will happen to the entire family. In its mythic imagination, Hong Kong might well blame mother England for not having taken it to bed with her, fulfilling its Oedipal desire, when she forced the father out. In Freudian terms, Hong Kong is portrayed here as trapped between two primal fears: castration by the father (as punishment for its antagonism to him and his desire for the mother) and symbolic self-castration (feminization, in pursuit of his favor). And, as in Freud's words, "both impulses, hatred of the father and being in love with the father, undergo repression": Hong Kong remains a colony (a child) arrested in its development, lacking any clear identity of its own, with only the limited options of protest and submission.[37] The ill-fated wheels going round in the opening scene (fig. 49) have come to this: bicycle turns back into wooden cart, son reverts to father, Hong Kong comes home to China. The father is dead, but with the death of the mother, the Father—the patriarchy, the so-called "Name of the father"—has been restored. As in Sophocles' *Oedipus at Colonus* and *Antigone*, female pollution is purged, and even as it is transferred laterally, the old male line of authority is reestablished (from Laius past Oedipus and his sons to Creon, or from Han Confucianists past the Manchus and Brittania to the Communists).[38]

The Day the Sun Turned Cold concludes with a written statement that projects the child's conflicted personality onto his audience: "After the case began, of more than one hundred letters which the son received, half praised him, and half condemned him."

CHAPTER 3

The Chinese Heart in Conflict with Itself:

Good Men, Good Women

. . . or shall I pretend that I am not myself, but somebody else strikingly like me, and look as though nothing were the matter. Just . . . not me, not me, and that's all.

—Feodor Dostoevsky, *The Double*

. . . time is dead as long as it is being clicked off by little wheels; only when the clock stops does time come to life.

—William Faulkner, *The Sound and the Fury*

Good Men, Good Women/Hao nan hao nü. Director: Hou Hsiao-hsien; Cinematography: Chen Hwai-en; Film editing: Chen Hwai-en, Liao Ching-Song; Music: Ku Chih-wen, Lin Shao-ying; Music supervision: Chen Hwai-en, Chiang Hsiao-Wen; Cast: Annie Shizuka Inoh (Liang Ching and Chiang Bi-Yu); Giong Lim (Chung Hao-Tung); Jack Kao (Ah Wei); Vicky Wei (Liang Shu-wen, Liang Ching's sister); King Jieh-wen (Liang Ching's brother-in-law); Tsai Chen-nan (Ah Ying); Lan Bow-Chow (Hsiao Dao-ying); Lu Li-chin (Mrs. Hsiao); Kao Ming (Lee Nan-feng); Screenplay: Chu T'ien-wen; Original text: Chiang Bi-Yu, Lan Bow-Chow (*Song of the Covered Wagon* [Huangmache zhi ge])[1]; Production: Mizuno Katsushiro, Ichiyama Shozo, King Jieh-wen, Ben Hsieh; Studio: 3H Films/Shochiku Films; 1995; 108 minutes

Good Men, Good Women

PLOT SUMMARY

This fragmented narrative is told in four voices covering three or four time periods: (1) the story of bar girl Liang Ching and her gangster boyfriend, Ah Wei, set in the near past; (2) Liang Ching, in the present, having become an actress after the gangland murder of Ah Wei but still wrestling with a troubled past in the form of her diary, pages of which are being faxed to her daily from an unknown source; (3) Chiang Bi-Yu, a historical figure and Taiwanese resistance fighter together with her husband, Chung Hao-Tung, during the War Against Japan, 1940–45, and the postwar years, as performed by Liang Ching in a film-within-the-film; (4) staged rehearsals, ambiguous in their temporal setting, for a documentary film about Chiang Bi-Yu, starring Liang Ching as Chiang. Altogether, there are twenty-five major shifts in time and voice, with sequences usually marked as striking shifts but often linked by significant thematic parallels.

The film opens as a film-within-a-film, with Chiang Bi-Yu, Chung Hao-Tung, and their companions arriving in Guangdong province to join the anti-Japanese resistance. Next, Liang Ching receives a fax referring to Ah Wei's death and a subsequent love affair by her. This leads to a scene in which Liang Ching and Ah Wei engage in a passionate romance in front of a mirror. Publicity shots are taken for the film-within-the-film. Rehearsal of Chiang and Chung's discussion of marriage and their plans to join the mainland resistance. Chiang Bi-Yu receives permission from her father to marry Chung Hao-Tung and go with him to the mainland, despite his warning that she'll pay a price for linking up with this socialist. Chiang, Chung, and their three Taiwanese companions arrive in Guangdong. Liang Ching receives a phone call from someone who doesn't answer and is again faxed the same diary page sent earlier, describing Liang Ching and Ah Wei's orgiastic New Year. Chiang, Chung, and companions are interrogated under suspicion of being Japanese conspirators and nar-

rowly escape execution. Liang Ching in her apartment ponders her situation. Liang Ching and Ah Wei discuss her pregnancy and whether to keep the baby. Chiang Bi-Yu, working as a nurse in the guerilla movement, is pregnant. Chiang and one of her Taiwan companions give up their babies for adoption so they can continue in the resistance movement. In the restaurant of her older sister, Liang Shu-wen, Liang Ching, her brother-in-law, and another gang member discuss a gang rivalry. Ah Wei struggles, in their New Year's retreat, to break Liang Ching of her drug addiction. Ah Wei meets with the rival gang at a dance hall and is murdered. Liang Ching, drunk and throwing up in her apartment beside a photograph of her portraying Chiang Bi-Yu. Japanese raiders steal food from Chiang Bi-Yu's resistance group. Rehearsal of a scene with Chiang Bi-Yu, Chung Hao-Tung, and comrades back in Taiwan after the war, discussing their socialist ideals and strategies, the Nationalist control of Taiwan, and the February 28, 1947, government massacre of Taiwanese intellectuals and activists. Chiang Bi-Yu is arrested by Nationalist soldiers in the government's repressive White Terror campaign of the early 1950s. Rehearsal scene of Chiang in prison. In prison, Chung Hao-Tung is carried, beaten and in chains, past Chiang's cell, from which young women prisoners are called forth for interrogation and possible execution. A badminton court, where Liang's sister accuses her of carrying on a relationship with her husband and fights with her, with their girlfriend Tong-Tong trying to stop them. A dance floor, where Liang, her sister, and Tong-Tong dance together and embrace, perhaps after their fight, perhaps after Ah Wei's murder. Liang Ching receives a phone call from someone who doesn't answer, admits accepting three million yuan from Ah Wei's murderers, and finally speaks to the caller as if he were Ah Wei. Chung Hao-Tung's name is posted among those executed. Chiang Bi-Yu's household receives news of the death. Next to Chung's body, Chiang burns offerings to his spirit, while his final letter to her is narrated in his voice. The film crew arrives in Guangdong, reprising the first scene of the film and announcing in Liang Ching's narration that Chiang Bi-Yu died the day before their departure from Taiwan at age seventy-four.

The Day the Sun Turned Cold opens with an image of machine-as-fate, a modern bicycle serving as a karmic juggernaut, filmed at the level of wheels and gears and pedals going around and leading mercilessly toward the doom that will envelop the film at its end. An unusual view, it reappears almost identically and with nearly identical purpose near the end of *Good Men, Good Women*, piercing the night and bearing a message of doom (figs. 49 and 65). An anonymous bicyclist rides through the darkness, only his feet seen at pedal level, heading toward a train station where he will post a list of those recently executed in the Taiwan government's secret campaign to exterminate "leftists." Lasting from 1950 to 1954, known as the White Terror (*baisi kongbu*), and carried on with the silent assent of the United States government, this campaign took as many as four thousand lives, mostly those of politically active intellectuals. On

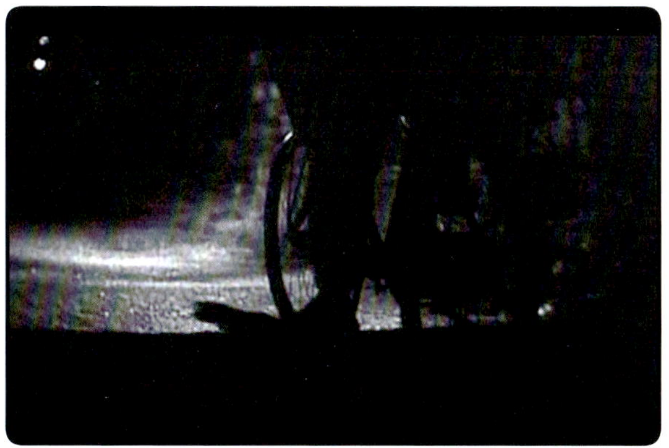

<table>
<tr><td>65</td><td>Good Men, Good Women, The Bicycle</td><td>66</td><td>Photographs of Chiang Bi-Yu (left, age sixteen, 1937) and Chung Hao-Tung (right) (from Lan Bow-Chow, Huangmache zhi ge)</td></tr>
</table>

the list of the executed was the name of *Good Men, Good Women*'s leading male figure, Chung Hao-Tung, an actual victim of this historical era. His widow, Chiang Bi-Yu (1921–95), survived imprisonment and possible execution to become a leading spokesperson in the early 1990s for bringing to light the nation's repressed history of this victimization and the forgotten memories of its victims (fig. 66).

Lou Ye's *Suzhou River* and Hou Hsiao-hsien's *Good Men, Good Women* both feature a "film-within-a-film." *Suzhou River* presents itself entirely as the work of its fictive videographer-narrator, who only gradually and quite unwillingly becomes a major part of—and ensnared by—the story he is telling. In *Good Men, Good Women*, a film actress increasingly desires to redefine her moral character in a kind of karmic reincarnation-without-death by exchanging her identity for that of the character she is performing—Chiang Bi-Yu—negotiating her way from film to film-within-film. Both *Good Men, Good Women* and *Suzhou River* work hard to chart and bridge the distance between fictional film and documentary, on the premise that by confessing its own fictionality to the audience, fictional film can establish for itself a deeper sense of authenticity—a convoluted logic by which film-within-film is presented as being more "real" than film itself. But neither of these films is limited to a narrow commentary on film itself, and in both films the blurring of boundaries between fantasy and reality has a purpose, an analog, in building a bridge between cultural inheritance and personal choice. The lead actress in each film performs two separate roles, and in each film this duality is explored internally by one of these characters herself as part of her quest to establish moral autonomy. Unlike Hitchcock's *Vertigo*, where separate female roles fuse and confuse only as a result of the hero's external manipulation, in *Suzhou River*, the adult Meimei explores and eventually adopts the child Mudan's naive faith in romantic love, while in *Good Men, Good Women*, Liang Ching does much the same with young Chiang Bi-Yu's commitment to guerilla patriotism.

In both cases, a male figure serves as an intermediary, a benign model, but not as manipulator. And in both cases, this moral fusion involves reaching back into the past to keep alive some better part of what tradition has to offer to a fissured society in search of its moral bearings.

For Hou Hsiao-hsien's Taiwan, as for William Faulkner's American South, "The past is never dead. It's not even past."[2] Liang Ching's rise from bar girl to actress resonates not only with Taiwan's own catapult from obscurity to economic international stardom but also with its morally troubled past, its mixed patrimony, the conflicting claims on its identity, and its tenuous hold on regional independence. As history shapes a nation, nations find it important to control the shape of their histories; yet being subject to so many divergent agendas, is it surprising that anything approaching a definitive textbook of Taiwan's history has yet to be written? Laying the groundwork for the "One China" policy which America and the People's Republic subscribe to today, Zhou Enlai once declared to Henry Kissinger, in 1971, "History . . . proves that Taiwan has belonged to China for more than 1,000 years."[3] But history could hardly be more different from that or Taiwan's identity more confused.

"Taiwan's isolation ends and its modern history begins in the sixteenth century," John Shepherd writes, with the arrival in aboriginal Taiwan of fishermen, merchants, and pirates from both Japan and China in the 1550s and with the "late arrival" in 1602 of the Dutch, "determined to break up Portuguese and Spanish monopolies of the China trade."[4] Before then, despite small numbers of Chinese fishermen who strayed to its shores, Taiwan was virtually a world unto itself. Soon afterwards, the rapid expansion and consolidation of Dutch rule was itself quickly ended as a result of internal mainland politics: at the fall of the Ming dynasty to the Manchu people's emerging Great Qing Empire in 1644–45, Chinese loyalists under Zheng Chenggong (known to the Dutch and to the West in general as Coxinga) established a Taiwan outpost in 1661 from which to maintain their resistance to the Manchus. In 1683, Zheng's successors were defeated by Qing forces, and a year later, after considerable debate at the Manchu court about whether assuming lasting control of the island was worth the responsibility it entailed, Taiwan was declared a prefecture of Fujian province. Taiwan thus first joined mainland Asia politically as part of the Manchu's Great Qing Empire, which had conquered and then controlled what today is called "China" and its "Han" Chinese population[5] and which would eventually cobble these together with Mongolia, northern Korea, northern Vietnam, parts of modern-day Russia, much of Central Asia, and Tibet. Much later, in 1886, in the declining days of the Manchu Empire, under increasing pressure from Spanish, Dutch, and Japanese interests operating there, Taiwan was granted separate provincial status for the first time. This rank was enjoyed for less than a decade. Well before Nationalist forces regained control of China from the Manchus in 1911, the island was already ceded by the Treaty of Shimonoseki in 1895 to the Japanese government as booty for their one-sided victory over Manchu forces the previous year. A Republic of Taiwan was proclaimed by a resistant portion of the local population but was readily overcome by the Japanese, and the next decades saw the widespread cultural, educational, and linguistic Japanization of the island. Not until the Japanese surrender to American forces in 1945 did the mainland government recover title to the island, and with the flight of this government in 1949, island and mainland were separated once again despite the rhetoric of unity perpetrated by such fictions as naming Taiwan city streets after towns and provinces on the mainland. Then, as *Good Men, Good Women* points out in its own way, with the outbreak of the Korean War in 1950 and the intensification of the Cold War in the Pacific, Taiwan became a military surrogate and economic colony of the United States.

Taiwan is a true island crossroads with a well-earned right to a profound identity crisis. Setting aside all political posturing, the outstanding fact remains that in its entire history, Taiwan has been controlled by a native Chinese mainland government for a total of less than five years, from 1945 to 1949. Most of those who live there now, or their forebears, arrived in successive waves of immigration, fought over and subdued Taiwan's native subjects and whoever else preceded them, and now, as the government withdraws its claims to mainland sovereignty and replaces "Republic of China" with "Taiwan" on its passports, their ancestral incursions are transformed historically from "civilizing missions" and liberating movements into the collective historical burden of an Orientals' Orientalizing.

In the pseudo-documentary portions of *Good Men, Good Women*, which are visually coded in black-and-white, very little actually happens by way of action. Rather, a situation, a condition is established. At the outset, the young intellectual Chiang Bi-Yu dresses[6] and speaks[7] Japanese. Chiang's father speaks in Japanese (fig. 67). This may go past an English-speaking audience unnoticed, but theirs is a largely Japanized culture. All Chinese dialects were prohibited then in public education, just as all local dialects would later be suppressed by the mainland Nationalist regime. Only her fiancé's experience as a student in Japan, where he was subjected to constant suspicion and surveillance, wakes him—and wakes her—to their separateness from Japan itself. And only when the couple makes its way to the mainland, to Guangdong province, does Chiang Bi-Yu regularly speak her native Taiwanese dialect, Hokkienese (roughly equivalent to mainland Fujianese). Yet there the couple can scarcely make themselves understood, and a translator is required for their Cantonese-speaking interrogator to understand them. When Chung Hao-Tung and his Taiwan compatriots are asked, repeatedly, why they have come, they stumble over a reply, partly because of the difference in language and partly over the fact that they are even being asked. Chiang Bi-Yu and Chung Hao-Tung have failed to calculate that in coming from Taiwan, they are regarded not as Chinese compatriots but as Japanese infiltrators. Arrested on arrival, it almost costs them their lives (fig. 68; *Good Men, Good Women* DVD, Scenes 2 and 3).

In the course of the film, various characters speak Japanese, Taiwanese (Hokkienese or Fujianese), Cantonese, Mandarin, and Hakka. They cannot understand each other

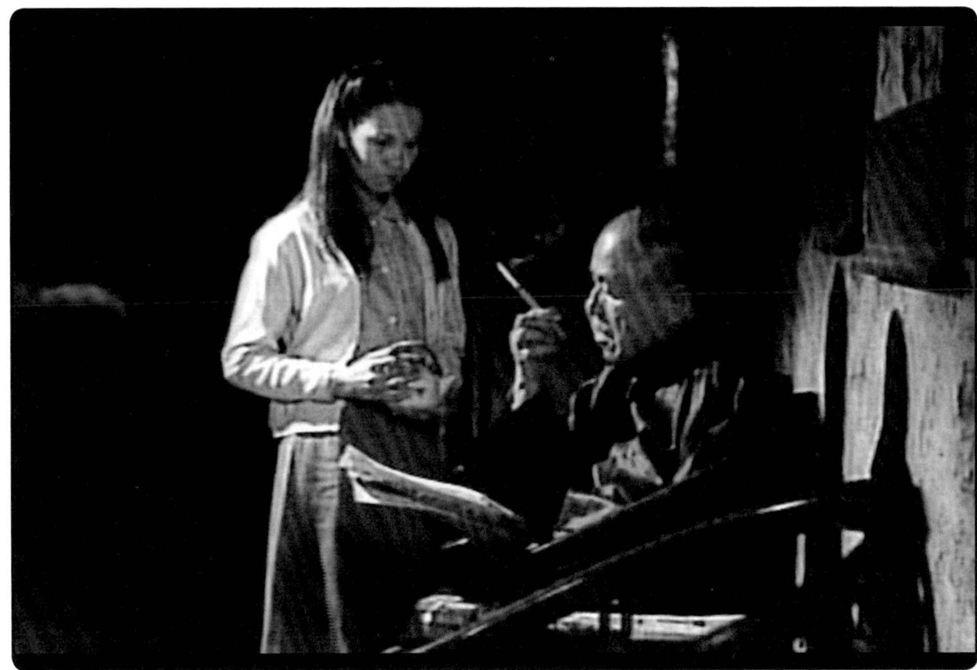

Good Men, Good Women, Chiang Bi-Yu and Father

and, of course, neither can the audience: for audiences everywhere, subtitles are a necessity.[8] For those in the film, the gulf between local dialects is like that between different countries. And then, when Chiang Bi-Yu and Chung Hao-Tung return to Taiwan after five years in the anti-Japanese resistance, they are once again regarded as aliens—Communists likely, bearers of a mainland ideological disease, and this time Chung pays with his life. Who takes his life? The ruling Nationalists, who have been likened to (and in no evident way contrasted with) Japan's mainland-invading imperialists. With the Nationalist regime still in power in 1995, when *Good Men, Good Women* was made, all these things remain unspoken in the film—or one might say they are "spoken" through this film's Babel of tongues—but the charge laid by the film at the feet of the Nationalist regime goes far beyond the charge of brutality and murder. By overturning—in the most fundamental, subliminal way—the *sense* of polyglot China as "one China," it fully labels the era of martial law as illegitimate.

Ironically, in the narrative blur produced through its multiple personalities and its interchangeable temporalities, *Good Men, Good Women* asserts its regional sympathies by way of a postcolonial idiom that de-legitimatizes consolidated authority, devalues unambiguous histories, and belittles singular outcomes as mere positivism. It does this even under the influence of a contrary tension, that of cultural globalization, and joins an increasing surge of popularity in recent Western films that disseminate a similar aesthetic, reducing fact and fiction to a rough equivalency.

68   *Good Men, Good Women*, Interrogation

Rosencrantz and Guildenstern Are Dead takes a fiction as its fact but renders each character as unstable as the Prince in his lunacy: two minor characters from *Hamlet* stumble out of the narrative role that Shakespeare has limited them to, yet in the end, after much deconstructing of Shakespeare and theater, they remain unable to alter the fate that Shakespeare has fixed for them. Films like *The Truman Show*, *The Matrix*, and *eXistenZ* suggest to the audience that our daily perceptions of reality are massive misperceptions, externally generated, and relocate our teleological position paranoically in a much grander, and horrific, scheme of things—requiring, of course, a heroic liberating gesture at the conclusions of their narratives. Alternate visions take on the appearance of reality in the minds of dying men in *Jacob's Ladder* and *The Sixth Sense*. In *The Player*, fictional characters mix with actors appearing under their own names, fiction turns into fact, and fact is turned into Hollywood "fiction." The German film *Run, Lola, Run* explores three widely divergent outcomes, given only minor ontological alterations along a primary narrative route. *Memento* explores through faulty memory its own *possible* narrative ontology in reverse sequence, trying to determine what *must* have set off its chain of events but revealing the fragility of any determinative knowledge given the gap between events and the recollection of them. The film reverts from its flawed "solution" to mere clues, and short of watching it backwards or managing to restructure it all backwards *in memory*, one is left with the same reality disorder as the flawed "hero."[9] David Lynch's *Lost Highway* represents a similar memory loop.[10] *Time Code* abandons singular time and place, screening four interrelated scenes at once for the full duration of the film. *Being John Malkovich* pokes postmodern fun at vicarious self-gratification—at the media-driven urge to "become" someone other than ourselves, especially when that someone else is rich and famous—by allowing this fantasy to actually take place (for Andy Warhol–like fifteen-minute intervals). Even the musicals play to this tune: *Chicago* stages Roxie's theatrical dreams as a series of fantasies within a fiction, but the fiction is based on a true story (first filmed in 1927). Of course, this play with multiple realities as represented by disintegrative personalities and fractured narratives is nothing new. *Blowup, The Conversation*, and *Zelig*, among others, represented this for a slightly earlier era, and before that, Alain Resnais's *Last Year at Marienbad*. A long history of this phenomenon in film can be delineated in both West and East, highlighted by the 1950 Japanese classic *Rashomon*, which has entered the English language as a synonym for parallax views of reality. Hitchcock indulged in this phenomenon frequently, dressing Norman Bates up as his own mother in *Psycho*, posing Judy as Madeleine (twice over) in *Vertigo*, producing multiple endings to the same film (*Topaz* and *Psycho*[11]), and even making the same film twice (*The Man Who Knew Too Much*).

Chinese-language films have not dabbled much with such multiple realities, but Yang Dechang's (Edward Yang's) pioneering film *The Terrorizer* (1986, Taiwan) goes a long way toward easing the boundary between events and perceptions by hopelessly confusing a frustrated mystery writer's "reality" with her warped fiction and by offering alternative but ambiguous endings.[12] *Ruan Lingyu* (Centre Stage/The Actress) (1992, Hong Kong) provides an exceptional film-within-a-film about filmmaking itself.[13] *Farewell My Concubine* (1993, PRC) explores the complex connections and disconnections between onstage and offstage personalities and performances.[14] *Farewell My Concubine*'s lead actor, female-impersonator Dieyi, experiences an almost total reversal of reality that is well described in the book on which the film is based, preferring the scripted life on stage to the uncontrollable tensions and unpredictable outcomes of real life:

> After all, life is just a play. Or an opera. It would be easier for all of us if we could watch only the highlights. Instead, we must endure convoluted plot twists and excruciating moments of suspense. We sit in the dark, threatened by vague menaces. Of course, those of us in the audience can always walk out; but the players have no choice. Once the curtain goes up they have to perform the play from beginning to end.[15]

Jiang Wen's *In the Heat of the Sun* (1994, PRC) pits diegesis against exegesis, subverting the monolithic control of "reality" by challenging and eventually undoing itself, just as it undoes the mythos of Communist heroics with which it is concerned. Deep into the film, the narrative suddenly comes to a literal, fixed-frame halt and the narrator proclaims,

Ha Ha! . . . Don't believe any of it. I never was this brave or heroic. I have kept swearing to tell the story truthfully, but no matter how strong my wish to tell the truth, all kinds of things have gotten in the way, and I sadly realize that I have no way to return to reality. My emotions changed my memories, which have in turn played with me and betrayed me. It got me all mixed up to the point where I can't distinguish between true and false.[16]

At this point, he begins to untell the story he has been telling. But as the confessed liar awkwardly stakes out his claim to the truth, the artificial sense of reality, sustained by cinematic style, now gives way to the higher reality of unreality, imbued with an awareness of the vulnerability of memory and truth. And so ironic when juxtaposed with *Good Men, Good Women*, the past here is fictionalized and imagined in color, while the fictionalizing present is shrouded in black-and-white.

The implicit thesis of Jiang Wen's film is nowhere better stated in simple terms than in Miklós Haraszti's account of artistic production in Soviet-controlled Hungary: "There is, in fact, only one taboo: the recognition of a *variety* of realities is forbidden, including any separate reality of one's own. . . . You do not need much theoretical training to realize that there can be no 'real' reality when there are many realities."[17] That taboo is violated by every fragmented time frame and every ambiguity, by every multiple character and multiple image described here. But such characters and images are hardly new. Like film-within-film, image-within-image has a long history in China, dating back almost two thousand years in the form of paintings (especially standing screens and, later on, hanging scrolls) depicted within paintings. This depiction of paintings as furnishings and as objects of contemplation was not at all uncommon, and at some point such paintings-within-paintings—perhaps when they became paintings-within-paintings-within-paintings, in the tenth century—drew conspicuous attention to the matter, elevating illusionism to the point of conscious focus and celebration[18] (fig. 69). In one well-known example, a painted subject sits in front of what may be another portrait of himself, with a painted landscape screen behind both of them.[19] And in another prominent work, one artist depicts his distinguished fellow artist Ni Zan (figs. 7 and 8) seated in front of a screen painting done in the style of the latter, and perhaps even executed by him,[20] constituting thereby a real painting posing as a simulacra (fig. 70). Since by this time an artist's work was often regarded as the image of his "true self"—imaging his character or personality as opposed to his phenomenal appearance—we have here yet another example depicting dual aspects of the same persona. Conceptually like cubist paintings, such works undermine the fixed point of reference and resist, deny, and subvert any expectation of narrative hegemony. Since both Daoism and Buddhism offered a sense of the "self" as ephemeral or wholly illusory, with religious illustrations to demonstrate this (such as the Daoist immortal Li Tieguai's acquired body seen exhaling his true, spiritual self[21]), Chinese artists were well prepared for a modern encounter with "the double" in Western

Zhou Wenju, attributed, Playing Chess in Front of the Double-Screen, Ming dynasty (?) copy of a tenth-century painting. Palace Museum, Beijing (from *Yiyuan duoying* 27)

Anonymous, *Portrait of Ni Zan*, ca. 1345. National Palace Museum, Taipei (from Wen Fong, *Possessing the Past*)

culture. However, what earlier Chinese cultural traditions offered, as suggested here, was based in personality and character, allowing for a blurring of the singular self via extensions into other forms and formats.[22] What it lacked was a psychodynamic dimension, a visual simultaneity of multiple selves generated from the conflicted desires and fears of an individual self worked out in complex narrative form.

Among Western doppelgängers there are plenty of precedents for doubles like Mudan and Meimei, who look alike but aren't, and yet whose likeness weaves their fate into a single narrative knot; or for Guan Jian, who perhaps *is* his fighting parents trapped in a single arrested-development psyche; and for the Liang Ching–Chiang

Bi-Yu fantasy relationship. For pre-cinematic prototypes of the look-alikes, one might think back to Alexandre Dumas's *The Man in the Iron Mask* or Mark Twain's later, lighter-hearted *The Prince and the Pauper*. Alternate personalities appear in Robert Louis Stevenson's *The Strange Case of Dr. Jekyll and Mr. Hyde* and Oscar Wilde's *The Picture of Dorian Gray*, and alternate realities occur in Ambrose Bierce's Civil War classic, "An Occurrence at Owl Creek Bridge." But for the definitive staging of double personalities and the thoroughgoing, internalized investigation of the uncertainty they represent one must turn to Dostoevsky, whose short novel *The Double* (1856) initiated a long run of such characters who would reappear in various "tones and styles" (as he phrased it) throughout his writing career.[23] The psychological multiplicity which Dostoevsky's figures endure is positively maddening: the initially liberating opportunity not to be one's one and only self is increasingly more than matched by the terrifying uncertainty of knowing no certain self. Here is Dostoevsky's original double, Golyadkin, at the original flowering of his duality:

> "To bow or not to bow? To hail him or not? To recognize him or not," our hero wondered in indescribable anguish, "or shall I pretend that I am not myself, but somebody else strikingly like me, and look as though nothing were the matter. Just . . . not me, not me, and that's all," said Mr. Golyadkin, taking off his hat to Andrey Filippovich, and keeping his eyes fixed on him. "Don't . . . don't mind me," he whispered with an effort; "just don't mind me. It's not me at all, Andrey Filippovich, it's not me at all, not me, and that's it."[24]

There is still a choice here, but once the pretence of social *choice* has vanished into an overdetermined psychic *condition*, once Golyadkin's psyche appears uncontrollably to have created someone *else* dressed up just like himself, the mind no longer poses limitations to reality or limits on fear: "'What's the meaning of it?' he [Golyadkin] thought with vexation. 'Why, have I really gone out of my mind?'"[25]

From the very outset of this creation, for which he drew almost compulsively on his own emergent hallucinatory and delusional experiences, Dostoevsky realized the potential inherent in the dual personality structure,[26] enabling him to explore through "inner narrative" the tension between personality formation (or deformation) and moral discovery, akin to what Faulkner so famously described as "the human heart in conflict with itself which alone can make good writing."[27] Dmitri Chizhevsky wrote of the moral dimension implicit in such doubles:

> The appearance of the double raises a question about the concreteness of man's real existence. It shows that simply "to exist"—"to be"—is not a sufficient condition for man's existence as an ethical individual. The problem of "stability," of the ontological "fixity" of an ethical being is the real problem of the nineteenth century.[28]

Once the presence of the double has been established on a detective-like basis, the moral search need not be limited to Dumasian look-alikes, morally contrasted, but may turn to other pairs—or even triplets—by means of whom the moral alternatives are set forth and the search is joined. For the realization of such existential instability, no less important than the pairing of Mudan and Meimei in *Suzhou River* is the tripling of (the virtually ever-present) Mada, the (barely seen) videographer, and the (wholly implicit) director. We cannot help but wonder just what is the relationship between Mada and the videographer or the relationship between the videographer and film director Lou Ye. Although they hardly seem like Mudan and Meimei (different people at first mistakenly and afterwards not mistakenly fated to become as one), the stalker Mada and the unnamed videographer appear like different expressions of the same being, alternative outcomes for the same predicament. In *choosing* not to take the path of his girlfriend Meimei—a kind of karmic pathway first blazed by the young Mudan (just a fiction to the videographer, or Mada's lie, until he views her dead body), who was followed sequentially by Mada and Meimei—the videographer defines *half* of Lou Ye. In choosing to present and emphasize two alternatives, Lou Ye strengthens his film, not tilting too strongly toward either of them. One alternative is ideal and almost surely the ideal audience's favorite; the other is a bitter reality, but cannot be dismissed. One cannot help but feel that most films, whether from Hollywood or Shanghai, would not resist making a feel-good choice between them (privileging Mada, that is), but part of what Lou Ye seems to acknowledge in resisting such a choice is the duality of his own cinematic identity and the moral compromise—the staging, the controlling manipulation, the intrusion—represented by filmmaking in general.

Good Men, Good Women is similarly—perhaps even more intensely—defined by doppelgängers, and this doubling takes on karmic overtones just as in *Suzhou River* (with Mada's descent into the waters of Suzhou Creek and his subsequent imprisonment: a moral death followed by his return as a new man, reborn with the soul and moral values of Mudan, supposedly dead, now implanted within him). Among the two (or three or four) characters performed by actress Annie Shizuka Inoh, actress-within-an-actress Liang Ching is a personality fissioned, morally contesting the lowly bar girl she used to be but unable to escape her own historical memory because (ostensibly) of the pages from her diary that are faxed to her daily from an unknown source, forced upon her as a reminder of the morally compromised basis of her present status. In contrast to Meimei's surveillance by her intrusive videographer boyfriend, Liang Ching is surveilled by her own past, as if her troubled conscience were externalized and mechanized in the form of a fax machine (fig. 71). At the outset, at least, she is no more able to break free from her own past corruption than she is able to escape the confines of her darkened, prisonlike apartment, and no freer than the goldfish swimming in a bowl next to her fax machine, a symbolic captive with which she plays while simultaneously captivated by the diary pages spewed out by her machine. Ironically, the same urban, upscale apartment and up-to-date gadgets that otherwise declare

71   *Good Men, Good Women, Fax*   72   *Good Men, Good Women, Ozu*

Liang Ching's escape from lower-class poverty also define a high-rise dungeon and shape her entrapment. She is isolated not merely from others but also darkly alienated from herself, from what in Chinese one might call her natural or moral self (*liangxin*). No one else ever appears in her apartment except as mediated by television, cinema posters, mirrors, and photography, and as figures understood only in relation to Liang Ching herself.

That Liang Ching is doomed to suffer daily reruns of her own past is mirrored by the cinematic rerun of Yasujiro Ozu's *Late Spring* (1949) playing on the television in her apartment, which sits beneath her fateful fax machine (fig. 72). The postwar Japanese woman seen there, performed by the smiling and all too cheerful Setsoku Hara, represents the same moment in time at which a far sadder Chiang Bi-Yu is to be performed by Liang Ching.[29] Although Liang Ching herself may not perceive this as the televised film runs its course, it constructs a painful irony, contrasting Japan's felicitous postwar revival with China's tragic postwar civil war. Whereas idealists like Chiang helped to liberate not only China but also Japan itself from the grip of Taisho-era Japanese militarism, in 1945 her native Taiwan fell only more deeply into the grip of militarists with its reversion to mainland Nationalist control, and even more so with the flight there in 1949 of the Nationalist government, which retreated before the Communist onslaught (*Good Men, Good Women* DVD, Scene 1).

Across the room from Ozu's *Late Spring*, the camera scans another telling cinematic image, a large advertising poster for the film *Blue Velvet*, featuring a split image of actress Isabella Rossellini[30] (fig. 73). Like the televised Ozu film, this carefully chosen reference further reveals the film's self-consciousness of its place in the world of cinematic arts. David Lynch's *Blue Velvet* describes the tenuous relationship, psychological and spiritual, between surface appearances and core realities, revealing the ordinary as unreal—a deceit, really—and presenting the surreal as deceptively real. Emphasizing the design features of this duality, the black-and-white poster derives

73 *Good Men, Good Women*, Poster   **74** *Blue Velvet*, The Door Opens

from the moment in the film when Rossellini's apartment is first penetrated—her psyche violated—by the naive protagonist, who hasn't the slightest idea yet of the dark corruption that lies within, but whose own vicarious urges deceive and drive him deeper and deeper into unknown and uncontrollable territory (fig. 74). Visible only briefly in *Good Men, Good Women* in a derivative medium, the presence of this cinematic art-within-art is sufficient to suggest the similar darkness that lurks within Liang Ching's own seemingly normal apartment. Compressed into this image is a cross-cultural reference to Liang Ching's own divided psyche and her compulsion to *become* rather than merely *perform* yet another identity, and to the ethnically and culturally divided but fused Taiwan personality, which all of this represents. Director Hou Hsiao-hsien's female unites within a single character all the innocence and corruption and frustrating confusion of Taiwanese identity that his friend and fellow filmmaker Yang Dechang similarly represents but typically distributes among a vast and bewildering cast of characters (*A Brighter Summer Day*, 1991; *Confucian Confusion*, 1994; *Mahjong*, 1996; *Yi Yi*, 2000).

Close by the Rossellini poster stands one more item, a mirror, which Liang Ching walks past just as this scene gives way to the next (fig. 73). Just as the poster is visually fragmented, Liang Ching's internal fragmentation is set forth graphically in the scene that follows, as she and her hoodlum boyfriend, backs to the camera, make love in front of a similar mirror (fig. 75; *Good Men, Good Women* DVD, Scene 1). Narcissistic, she fondles herself just as intently as he does.[31] Like the couple itself, the audience may be seduced by the illusion of beauty seen in the reflection, while the actual couple remains silhouetted in darkness and so shaded around the disappearing edges of the film frame that they are readily overlooked, blending into the darkness of the theater audience like the couple sitting in front of you. The loving couple, further coupled by the mirror, sees itself in the lighted glass just as the audience sees them, dimming the perceptual boundary between audience and characters-as-audience, or alternatively, making the discriminating audience aware of the artificial boundaries and the inexact contrast between surface and depth. It is notably difficult to focus on both images, real and reflected, at the same time.

75   *Good Men, Good Women, The Mirror*

This trope draws upon a deeply rooted tradition, a Chinese doppelgänger equivalency. What occurs in the mirror is not the same as the three-dimensional world it mimics, so what dimension *does* it reflect? Throughout Chinese literary history, moral criticism has been likened to a mirror reflecting an inner, numinous reality as opposed to one's superficial, phenomenal image. The *jian*, or burnished metal mirror, gives rise to the extended definition "A mirror of metal. To examine. To scrutinize; to criticise. An example or precept."[32] Zhang Hua's moralizing text *Admonitions of the Court Instructress*, from the year 292, includes the well-known passage "People all know how to perfect their appearance but none know how to adorn their character," which is illustrated in one of the oldest surviving Chinese paintings on silk, attributed to Gu Kaizhi, of the fourth century (fig. 76). While Zhang's text makes no mention of mirrors, the metaphoric linkage of inner character and moral scrutiny to the mirror is already so fixed by that period that the artist illustrates Zhang's phrase in reverse by a pair of court ladies making themselves up in front of bronze mirrors. An educated Chinese audience can scarcely watch Liang Ching cavorting in front of a mirror that reflects her behavior and literally *speculates* on her character without an awareness of the same negative inference. One almost expects, Dorian Gray–like, for the image to reflect and reveal the inner corruption that the beautiful bodies and faces disguise. (One experiences the same thing in *Vertigo*, seeing Judy at her mirror making herself up as someone she isn't; *Vertigo*'s Judy and *Suzhou River*'s Meimei both appear in

76 Gu Kaizhi, attributed, *Admonitions of the Court Instructress*, section, original ca. 400. British Museum, London (from *Zhongguo meishu quanji* 1)

their makeup mirrors as double-doubles, particularly unreal[ized] people who need—or for whom the audience needs—to discover their "true" selves.) It is interesting that grammatically the Chinese measure-word for mirror is *mian,* or "face," which further links the mirror to moral reputation and prestige (as in "saving face," *bao mian* or *liu mian,* and "losing face," *diu mian*).

As a moral tool, despite the fleeting nature of its reflections, the mirror became a trope for the historical record itself, the past as a moral mirror for the present, as used in the title of Sima Guang's *Comprehensive Mirror for the Aid of Good Government* (Zi zhi tong jian, 1084), and in painting, Tang Hou's *The Mirror of Paintings, Past and Present* (Gu jin hua jian, ca. 1330) and Xia Wenyan's *The Precious Mirror of Painting* (Tuhui bao jian, 1365).[33] The more recent glass mirror (*jing*) not only carries all the same, older connotations, it also intersects the world of film—*jingpian* is a lens; *jingtou* a camera lens or a cinematic scene; *chang jingtou* a long take or a distant shot—and infuses cinema with the same morally reflective capacity, or imperative, as the traditional concept of "mirroring" does with history itself.

77 *Good Men, Good Women,*
The Actress' Mirror

78 *Good Men, Good Women,*
Drunken Liang Ching

Notably, when bar girl Liang Ching becomes the actress Liang Ching after the murder of her boyfriend Ah Wei, a similar mirror at first appears significantly in her new, upscale urban apartment (fig. 77), beside which is soon placed a photograph of Chiang Bi-Yu, or rather a Liang Ching publicity photo *as* Chiang Bi-Yu. Like Jacques Lacan's concept of "the child's mirror image as the model and basis for its future identifications,"[34] Liang's maturing ego is measured here by the shift from a *reflection* of her libidinal narcissism to her *depiction* of a social ideal that she increasingly identifies with at the same time as she increasingly recognizes her distance from it. This photographic simulation is not easily matched by a moral transformation, and the first scene where this Liang-as-Chiang photo appears (the photographing of it having been shown earlier in the film) is one that slowly and painfully displays a falling-down-drunk Liang Ching throwing up beside it (fig. 78). It is a poor reflection on Liang Ching's character, but a reminder of the miseries she has had to face coming up the hard way, as a prostitute and drug addict, compared to the politically courageous but privileged, well-educated, and virginal young Chiang Bi-Yu. Nonetheless, to the degree that she is intended to analogize Taiwan culture, as Liang herself seems to step backward in time from a self-indulgent present (her own) to a self-sacrificing past (Chiang Bi-Yu's), the audience is obliged to consider what ideals and what reality this step is based on. Was the Taiwan of the past (fighting for causes, but battle torn nonetheless) really so much more noble than the Taiwan of the present (indulging in the fruits of peace, and perhaps morally adrift), or is Hou Hsiao-hsien simply prone to nostalgia? Are the loftier ideals of the past really recoverable, or even relevant, in the present? Is Liang's newfound ideal a valid identity or simply a more sophisticated expression of her narcissism? Could this even mask an unconsciously contrived death wish on the part of the deeply grieving Liang Ching (or Hou Hsiao-hsien, grieving for the lost Taiwan of his childhood)?[35] Such considerations and conundrums are not resolved but, rather, remain on stage as persistent alternatives to any cinematic closure, which by the standards

79 *Good Men, Good Women*, Mirror-Ball

80 *Good Men, Good Women*, Arrival

of this film would be mechanical and artificial. These double images, therefore, remind us on the one hand that images deceive, that an actress may be just an actress and a character just a fiction; on the other hand they suggest that just as the dual function of a frame is both to separate *and* to attach one thing to another (a mirror, a precious painting, a filmed image to a wall), the framed image here is both separated from *and* connected to the larger world, attaching the flawed Liang Ching to the lofty ideal of Chiang Bi-Yu. What drives Liang toward this ideal is never revealed; her character is never that transparent. Rather, this drive is embedded in the doubled-image as dramatized by the doubled-structure of film-within-film.

Add to this refractive imagery the multifaceted mirror-ball that Ah Wei introduces as visual spice to the couple's weekend orgy (fig. 79), a borrowed symbol of public spectacle and abandoned integrity associated with Western-style ballroom dancing in Shanghai during the 1920s and 1930s. While its origins are Western, from a period notable for its "roaring" excess, such a fragmented surface could only reflect in the Chinese imagination an ominously fractured image, and indeed, its later appearance in the film lights up Ah Wei's ignominious death on a dancehall floor (fig. 88). Finally, just as the Chinese "mirror" often assumed a literary format, it is as a parallel to these spectral images that Liang's fax machine daily offers a text-based mirror of Liang's earlier life, reflections not across space but over time, thrusting the moral and karmic consequence of past deeds and misdeeds into the present.

All these mirrored fragments resonate with the disrupted temporal structure of the film, which similarly binds together people who are otherwise enclosed in different time frames and who seem otherwise isolated in separate moral spheres. And rather than being extruded in a linear temporal sequence, the narrative sequence can be visualized as a series of rapid leaps from one time period to another, generated by straightforward motion along a spiralling braid woven from multiple narrative-temporal strands. Two of these narrative strands are unambiguous as to time and persona. These include Liang Ching in the present, an actress, and Liang Ching in the near past, as a bar girl and mistress to the gangster Ah Wei, both of which are shown in color. The third strand is usually seen in sepia-toned black-and-white, cinematic coding for a more distant past and ambiguously depicting the Taiwanese resistance fighter Chiang Bi-Yu as performed by the contemporary actress Liang Ching, with an occasional gradual resaturation from black-and-white into color. A fourth element consists of rehearsal scenes, shown in color. If one takes the scenes with Chiang Bi-Yu for what they most readily appear to be—past tense—then the sequence of shifts in time throughout the film has an interesting and fairly simple logic about it (charting the present as 1, the near past as 2, and the distant past as 3, and reading vertical columns in sequence from left to right, 3-1-2-3-1-2-3 . . .):

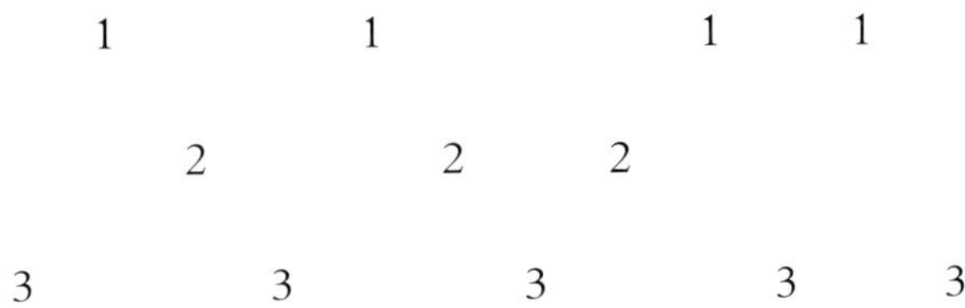

We begin and end in exactly the same spot (the arrival in Guangdong in 1940; fig. 80), leading at the outset *to* the present (Liang Ching receiving a fax) and arriving in the end *from* the present (Liang Ching, again, receiving a fax). A series of regular present to near past to distant past sequences (1-2-3) occupy most of the film, with an exceptional past to near past to present step (3-2-1) leading to a present to distant-past double cadence at the conclusion. The sequencing, on paper, looks almost musical by Western standards, like an elegant minuet beginning on the upbeat, but the 3-3 opening-closure return provides a distinctive and sublime resolution, like that of Bach's *Goldberg Variations,* the Requiem/Kyrie and Lux aeterna/Cum sanctis tuis of Mozart's *Requiem,* and Beethoven's Piano Sonata op. 109. The full sequence, however, as laid out here, depends on our treating the rehearsal scenes for what they *represent* (which is always Chiang Bi-Yu in the distant past), rather than for what they *are.* But the rehearsal scenes are more ambiguous, more complex than that: shown in color, as opposed to the "finished" sepia-toned film-within-the-film, they constitute yet another cinematic space (fig. 81). Moreover, the final scene—which is literally the first scene of the film repeated, first shown in a desaturated black-and-white and then shown a second time in color—is understood in its first iteration to be the historical past and in its reiteration becomes another present-day re-creation, not unambiguously then or now, but another staging or rehearsal. If we differentiate all these rehearsal scenes as a voice set in the *filmic* present tense, then an extended and more complex series emerges (rehearsals here are marked as R and placed in the non-filmic or documentary present):

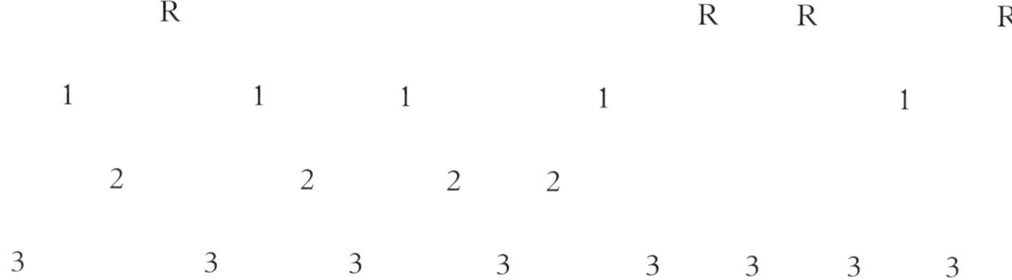

There is no graceful minuet here, especially if we acknowledge the temporal duality of the rehearsal scenes. Time here is becoming increasingly fractured, like a broken mirror. However, this is by no means the end of the film's chronological ambiguities. The rehearsal scenes *might* represent Liang Ching (in the filmic present) practicing her role as Chiang Bi-Yu—we can see the filmmakers looking on. But these scenes might equally well represent Annie Shizuka Inoh and Hou Hsiao-hsien rehearsing *her* role (as Liang Ching as Chiang Bi-Yu)—in other words, rather than depicting a fictive preparation for the pseudo-documentary *Good Men, Good Women*, these scenes might instead construct, in neutral voice, a real documentary in real time about the making of *Good Men, Good Women*. The film, then, would include fiction, pseudo-documentary, and authentic documentary elements. This unfolding raises the questions: for actors, when does acting begin and end, what mediating role does rehearsal play, and who is *not* an actor?

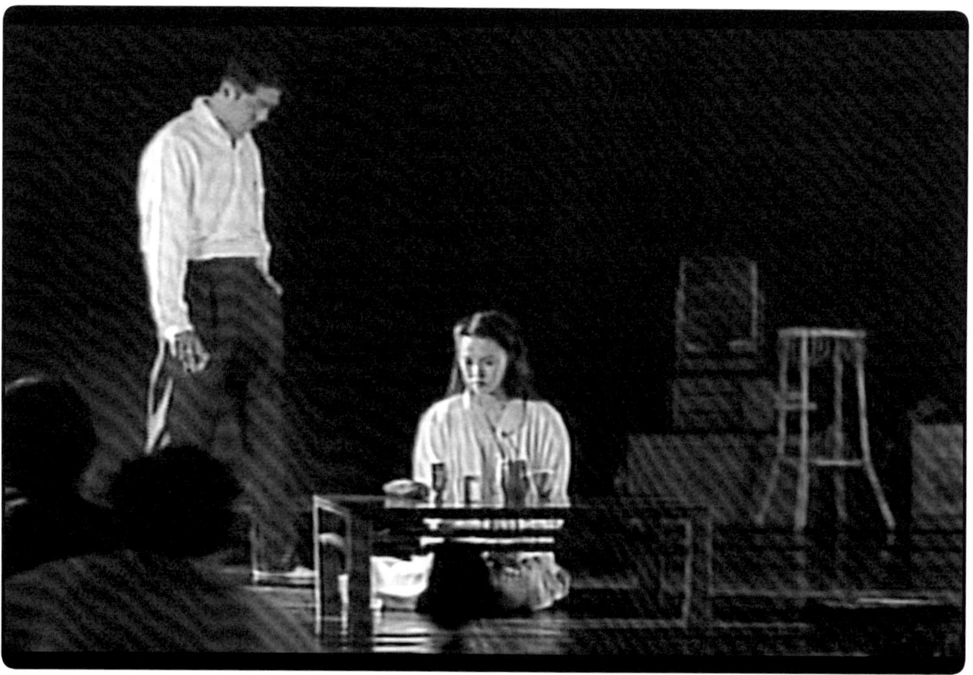

81　*Good Men, Good Women*, Rehearsal

The viewers' task of locating events in time is complicated and enriched by the addition of Liang Ching's carefully coordinated voice-over narratives, which link the present with both the near and distant past, as well as by faxes that come out of the near past to haunt Liang Ching in the present. Rather than being provided with some entropic mechanism to reduce all this to a more stable and comprehensible pattern, the viewer is obliged to experience the outwardly spiralling force and complexity of these scenes. I will not try again to chart all this on the page in its fullest realization, like some musical notes on a staff. A Western musical analogy for this, if there is one, would come best from the likes of Bach's grand passacaglias, or especially from the closing movements of Beethoven's *Hammerklavier* and his final sonata, op. 111, great polyphonic works best listened to as "summas" that search for nobility amidst the muck of human tragedy and slowly, painfully attain it. Traditional Chinese music provides no equivalent.

Since Liang Ching is herself a fictional creation while Chiang Bi-Yu is introduced to the audience at the outset as a genuine historical figure, the audience is left to puzzle over the case of a fiction portraying a reality. Fictional Liang Ching is even described as meeting the real Chiang Bi-Yu during filmmaking, visiting her in the hospital, and indeed the real Chiang Bi-Yu *was* then in the hospital; the person who would have met her there was the real-life actress Annie Shizuka Inoh, but Liang narrates how an ailing Chiang Bi-Yu told her that she looks like Chiang used to (and "she was very pretty then"). "We've been rehearsing for a month now," Liang Ching says at one point. "Wonder when we'll start shooting. I feel as if I'm turning into Chiang Bi-Yu" (*Good Men, Good Women* DVD, Scenes 2 and 3). These, of course, are impossible thoughts thrust credibly into the audience's head: that the black-and-white film it has already been watching hasn't been shot yet, and that real people are turning into fictional characters while fictional characters are turning into real ones. The audience is let loose in a cinematic fun house, but not for fun. These contrivances aren't merely avant-garde formalities; they blur the definitional edges of "reality" so that something softer and more important can be advanced: the increasing attraction of Liang to Chiang and the dissolution of boundaries between the actual and the potential. Reversing course, they establish the possibility for the already living to become reincarnated as the already dead. As the film ends, exactly where it began but now in color, what once had been Chiang Bi-Yu is now Liang Ching, and the fictional Liang announces the sad fact that real Chiang Bi-Yu can never see the result, having died the day before filming began on the mainland.[36] Is the transformation complete, or only beginning, or is it simply imagined? What author-director Hou seems to insist upon here is our viewing life itself as an art form.

Where else does one find such an elaborate and purposeful fracturing of narrative sequence? Perhaps Jan Potocki's obscure but quintessentially baroque novel *The Manuscript Found in Saragossa*, filmed by Wojciech Has (1965), "a novel of frames"[37] which Salmon Rushdie describes as "constructed like a Chinese box of tales"[38] and a (pseudo) manuscript-within-a-manuscript, which its psychologically troubled Polish author continuously composed, elaborated, and republished for years up to the time of his suicide in 1815. Still, for a study of fractured time, interpenetrating tenses, and history as a timeless morality tale, perhaps one turns best to William Faulkner, and the young Faulkner at that: his then-revolutionary and deeply Freudian *The Sound and the Fury* (1929, published at age thirty-two). Surprisingly like *Good Men, Good Women*, *The Sound and the Fury* is written in three subjective voices (two unambiguous, one ambiguous as to the perception of time) and a fourth "neutral" one. As Hou Hsiao-hsien's film relies on voice-overs, faxes, and contrasts of color with black-and-white to confuse and clarify his narrative structure, Faulkner required italics and Roman type and also wanted to use different colored inks to help steer the audience through the novel's various voices and times.[39] Faulkner defied his readers (who were precious few at the time) to puzzle out exactly where they were at any "one moment" in time, as if there *were* such singular moments, and to grasp what his sequences signified.[40] Similarly, the (small and disappointed) audience's difficult task in navigating the complex structure of *Good Men, Good Women* and in earning the rewards this effort has to offer—a task even more demanding in the medium of film than it would be for readers—has been held to account for its becoming perhaps the least well received among Hou Hsiao-hsien's major films.[41]

But the challenge of these works to their audience is not merely gratuitous. Jean-Paul Sartre wrote that time itself was what *The Sound and the Fury* was really all about: "Man's misfortune lies in his being time-bound. . . . Such is the real subject of the book. And if the technique Faulkner has adopted seems at first a negation of temporality, the reason is that we confuse temporality with chronology."[42] To a degree, Faulkner backed Sartre up, writing that "time is dead as long as it is being clicked off by little wheels; only when the clock stops does time come to life."[43] But for Faulkner, unlike for Sartre, time was given a moral purpose. Faulkner's South (much like Hou Hsiao-hsien's Taiwan) was out of joint with the times and uncertain about its relation to the larger geographic sphere to which it forcibly belonged (bound by a history of military conquest), unable to abandon its troubled past, unwilling to forsake its difference, and unready to write its own history.

Faulkner, for whom the South had its own history to teach and its own moral tale to tell, rejected the singularity—the absolutism—of time. Liberated from predictable linear sequence, time for Faulkner, as for Hou Hsiao-hsien, became an artistic construction by which to describe history itself as opaque and unpredictable, as a narrative of meaningful choices made under unpredictable conditions of ever-changing moral circumstances and therefore requiring an elasticity of moral judgment. What Faulkner emphasized (to the dismay of many Northern intellectuals), and what *Good Men, Good Women* offers (another major reason, I believe, for its relatively poor reception), is a profound but surprisingly flexible and forgiving moral voice.[44] If the past is not yet past, as Faulkner wrote, then one is never external to it but forever living with it, and where then is its clear mirror? Rather than offering a judgmental standard of morality firmly fixed by a fixed past, Faulkner's fluid time sense emphasized the moral struggle of living *within* history, contemplating but not condemning, "suspending judgment." Faulkner's *Absalom, Absalom!* tells a lurid tale of greed and prejudice that encapsulates the moral problems of Southern history, likened by its title to the Biblical sins of King David but concluding with the storyteller's responding to the question, "just tell me one thing more. Why do you hate the South?" (as the Lord himself might have responded to a similar question about his badly flawed but much favored David), *"I dont. I dont! I dont hate it! I dont hate it!"*[45] Like Faulkner, who ended up on the wrong side of history, Hou Hsiao-hsien offers a similar sensibility, a striking departure from traditional Chinese moral certainties (whose classic occurrences range the chronological spectrum from Confucius' "rectification of names" to Buddhism's principles of karmic inheritance to Mao Zedong's pseudo-Hegelian "permanent revolution") and a rejection of all those opportunities provided by time and man to hate and condemn any and all of those who were party to Taiwan's convoluted fate: the Japanese, the Nationalists, the Communists, the soldiers, profiteers, and gangsters, and those whose invasion of the island took collective advantage of all those who came before and then proved unable or unwilling to resist all those and all that which came afterwards. In Hou Hsiao-hsien's moral universe, which bears witness to the contrasts of circumstance that time and fate visit undeservedly upon otherwise interchangeable individuals, self-righteousness and retribution have no proper place, while pity and compassion take a lofty place alongside of those things worthy of honor and pride.

In addition to the question already raised by the patriot Chiang Bi-Yu: to whom—if not itself—does Taiwan "belong," is added the question by actress Liang Ching: how does modern Taiwan relate to itself and to its own moral heritage? Spiritually aimless and morally adrift, how do hoodlum Ah Wei and bar girl Liang Ching (she who collected hush money from his murderers, buying her way out of poverty at the everlasting cost of his reputation and perhaps of her own soul[46]) represent the cause and the heritage that Chung Hao-Tung and Chiang Bi-Yu fought for so bravely, so selflessly? What moral indifference has modern Taiwan come to that its hard-won peace and newfound prosperity apparently cannot mediate? And what is it that relates these two characters and these two questions? As with Faulkner, with Hou Hsiao-hsien the moral purpose is lodged in the intensely structured use of time. With its voice-overs, fax deliveries, and rehearsals that bridge the interspersed time periods, a kind of temporal Babel seems to reign in *Good Men, Good Women* that reinforces the disconnectedness of sound (dialect) and place (Taiwan, China, Japan) and intersects with them in such a way as to dispossess anyone and everyone of clarity and priority, of linguistic, political, and moral privilege. At one point a drunk and probably drugged Liang Ching sings on stage ("All around I see gilded lives / But mine is tarnished. . . . Why was I born under a bad star?") at the same time that she and Ah Wei are shown on the

82 *Good Men, Good Women,*
Pregnant Liang Ching

83 *Good Men, Good Women,*
Pregnant Chiang Bi-Yu

dance floor, where he is shot to death in her arms. And yet, this chaotic leveling force of time and history carries with it an elevating moral logic, defined here not by uniqueness of place and privilege but by juxtaposition. The narrative feature that delivers *Good Men, Good Women* from sheer narrative babble and provides its profound cinematic voice is the meticulous pattern of temporal sequences that suture together a revealing set of moral contrasts and identities:

84 *Good Men, Good Women*, Publicity Photo

85   *Good Men, Good Women*, "Taiwan Is under Japanese Control"

• the cinematic cut from a pregnant Liang Ching, with a self-centered Ah Wei making assumptions about male offspring ("a little Ah Wei") and his own paternity (to which she replies "I am a bar hostess, you know") and discussing whether *he* really wants the child or not // to the pregnant Chiang Bi-Yu, working stoically as a nurse in the resistance camp shortly before abandoning her child to adoption in order to continue the patriotic work (figs. 82 and 83);[47]

• the cut from Liang Ching performing steamy romance with Ah Wei in front of a mirror // to Liang Ching performing as Chiang Bi-Yu in front of a camera's lens (figs. 75 and 84);

• the cut from Chiang Bi-Yu's group greeted in Guangdong by a display of widespread suspicion about their background, with no way even of speaking directly to their interrogators // to the scene of Liang Ching receiving anonymously faxed pages of her diary that cast suspicion on her moral background, with no way to address her accuser (figs. 85 and 71);

• Ah Wei discussing gangland deals in a dance hall meeting, resulting in his murder // compared with Chung Hao-Tung's ideological group discussing socialist strategy, which leads to his political murder (figs. 86–89; *Good Men, Good Women* DVD; Scenes 4 and 5;)

• Liang Ching drunk and vomiting by a portrait of (herself as) Chiang Bi-Yu //
followed immediately by Chiang's resistance group having its meager food supply
stolen by a Japanese raiding party (figs. 78 and 90);

• from the Taiwan prison, where the inhumanity and suffering are made all the
more painful to witness by the quiet way in which the victims bond together and
silently accept their fate // to the cut of a fancy indoor badminton court that resembles a similarly bunkered scene refurbished in modern times, where the titanic ideological struggles of the past give way in the throes of affluence to unwarranted jealousy and intra-family bickering, like some karmic inheritance expressing a natural propensity to struggle and fight even when one can no longer find a meaningful cause to fight for (figs. 91–93);

• the juxtaposition of Liang Ching, seated before a portrait of Chiang Bi-Yu and
Chung Hao-Tung, speaking to her anonymous caller as if he were the ghost of Ah Wei
("I've visited your grave every year") and confessing her betrayal of him // followed
by the announcement of Chung Hao-Tung's execution, then by Ching Bi-Yu's burning of sacrificial offerings to his deceased spirit (figs. 94 and 100);

• the death of Chung Hao-Tung, set in the past and mourned by Chiang Bi-Yu (as
performed by Liang Ching) // followed seamlessly by the arrival of the acting crew in
Guangdong to film the mainland scenes in which Liang Ching in the cinematic
"present" announces in voice-over the death of Chiang Bi-Yu at the age of seventy-four (figs. 100 and 80; *Good Men, Good Women* DVD, Scene 5);

• the identification, in the initial and final scenes of the film, of the film crew with
the patriots they perform, arriving in Guangdong to film the scenes of anti-Japanese
resistance, the difference between them no longer distinguishable (fig. 80).

All this is not merely plot logic but a poignant evocation, sometimes wrenchingly
painful to behold as it measures the older world, with its profound political woes but
heroic sense of purpose, against the modern Taiwan revolution, with its wealth and its
anomie. The times have changed, but what of human nature? Are the generations

86   *Good Men, Good Women,*
Gangland Banquet

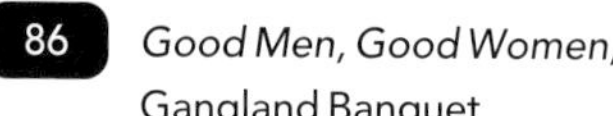

87   *Good Men, Good Women,*
Land Reform Meeting

actually all that different, and what really can be held to account for change and change-lessness? Is it the case that people *need* to suffer primal hardships in order to find their better selves?

88 *Good Men, Good Women,*
Ah Wei Dead

89 *Good Men, Good Women,*
Chung Hao-Tung Dead

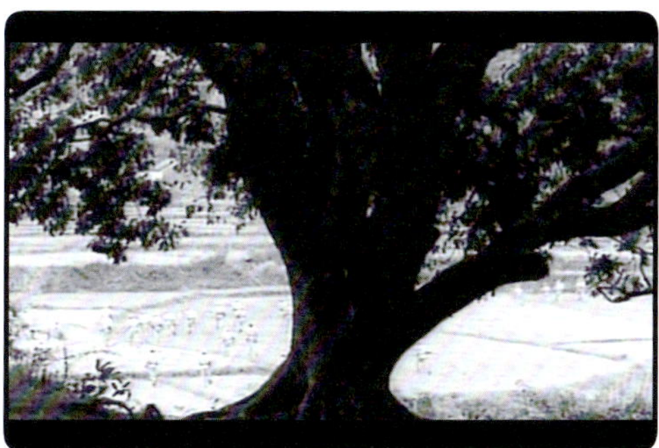

90 *Good Men, Good Women,*
Japanese Raid

91 *Good Men, Good Women,*
White Terror Prisoners

92 *Good Men, Good Women,*
Taiwan Prison

93 *Good Men, Good Women,*
Badminton Court

94 *Good Men, Good Women, Confession*

Like a great many artists, Hou Hsiao-hsien prefers not to offer much verbal insight into his creation. His scriptwriter Chu T'ien-wen writes sympathetically, "If an artist doesn't want to explicate his own work, it's because he has already said what he wants to say in the work itself and any explanations or interpretations will all be superfluous 'hindsight.'"[48] Four months after beginning his now-published filming notes, Hou entered the following: "I've been thinking more and more about *Good Men, Good Women:* the real point of it lies in becoming more *authentic* in human affairs."[49] Absent privilege, leveled by historical fate, but not free of history or beyond morality, what remains for the moral individual to strive for is this "authenticity."

In a documentary film about him, *HHH: Portrait of Hou Hsiao-Hsien,*[50] Hou states, "The composing of my characters . . . I got my ideas for my films from people [performers, that is]. There are Kao Chieh, Li T'ien-lu, Annie Shizuka Inoh, Wu Nienjen. First you have these people, then you develop your stories around them. It begins with people. . . . *Puppetmaster* was about Li and his family [Li T'ien-lu, Taiwan's official national-treasure puppeteer, both star and subject of the film]. *Good Men, Good Women* was about Annie Shizuka Inoh and her contemporaries' viewpoint. *Goodbye South, Goodbye* followed because I wanted to elaborate more on these contemporaries, their wit, their ideas and tempo." Chu T'ien-wen confirms the notion: having developed the cinematic long take as a realistic device, Hou has long avoided using movie stars in favor of "natural" talent and prefers distant shots to facilitate the work of nonprofessional actors. And Hou, claims Chu, had kept his sights set on Annie Shizuka Inoh since 1988, when he decided she wasn't yet ready for the role of Hiromi in Hou's earlier film, *A City of Sadness* (1989). Once he decided she was ready, he set about building a story line that would best display Inoh's diverse talents. The plot, writes Chu, was secondary to the presence of Inoh. (Liang Ching even seems to be named for Annie Shizuka Inoh, the written character for "Shizuka" in Japanese being "Ching" in Chinese.) Having pushed the long take and narrative storytelling to its limits in *The Puppetmaster* (1993), he now wanted to try something different, something more complex, and the story line underwent numerous radical changes before arriving at its final form.[51] There are parallels here to Faulkner's description of how *The Sound and the Fury* began with the single image of a central female (climbing a tree as a bold young girl with symbolically "muddy drawers" to spy through a window on the adults at a family wake, conceived as "a short story, something that could be done in about two pages, a thousand words, [but] I found out it couldn't") and evolved into a complex narrative written and rewritten in the different voices of its main characters (becoming more and more "elastic . . . until it covered the whole family" and ultimately "took the rest of the four hundred pages to explain").[52]

The evolution of *Good Men, Good Women* also took some surprising and complicated turns. Hou's *A City of Sadness* focused on the transition from Japanese to Chinese control of the island, breaking the public silence about the Nationalist government's massacre of island intellectuals, which began with an incident on February 28, 1947 (now popularly called "2-2-8") and, at the cost of as many as thirty thousand lives, helped to secure the reimposition of mainland China's control after the Japanese departure. This film was followed by *The Puppetmaster,* which focused on artistic life earlier in the century, during Japanese colonization.[53] Conceptualizing a third film to complete his "Taiwan history project," Hou planned a film that would deal with the Nationalist government's White Terror campaign, which gathered force after the Korean War began and the United States reinstituted its prior policy of protecting Taiwan from possible Communist attack.[54] Hou planned at first to film a novel by Chu T'ien-hsin, the sister of his regular scriptwriter Chu T'ien-wen. The novel, *Long, Long Ago There Was a Man Called Urashima Taro* (Congqian congqian you ge Urashima Taro), is based on a Japanese fairytale found in such ancient sources as *Yuryaku-ki, Man'yo-shu, Tango Fudo-ki*, and *Urashima ko-den*. In the original, a fisherman from Urashima releases a turtle he has caught, which in gratitude takes him to the underwater palace of the dragon king, where he remains for what seems like a day. On his departure, he is given a jeweled box with the instruction never to open it, but on his return he opens the box, which turns him into an old gray man in a world so changed he cannot recognize it. This Rip van Winkle–like tale was designed to "describe the old government's resistance to social change,"[55] while it also captured the predicament of the government's victims, trapped in memory by social repression or simply forgotten after the island's rapid march to modernity began. However, Chu T'ien-wen says it was because Hou wanted to feature pop star Annie Shizuka Inoh that he abandoned this story in favor of material from Lan Bow-Chow's *Song of the Covered Wagon* (Huangmache zhi ge), an oral history based on interviews of White Terror survivors, which Hou had previously used in making *A City of Sadness*.[56] Lan's book—named after a Japanese song that was sung by imprisoned victims of the February 28 Incident and is heard in *A City of Sadness*—was largely inspired by Chiang Bi-Yu's campaign to resurrect the memory of the White Terror and includes the story of Chiang and Chung Hao-Tung. A considerable transformation of this material by Hou and scriptwriter Chu T'ien-wen was required to produce the film. At the same time, Hou Hsiao-hsien also funded a documentary about the White Terror by a film team that included Lan Bow-Chow entitled *Why Don't We Sing* (1995), named for the song which begins and concludes *Good Men, Good Women*—a combination of document and fiction parallel to that *within* the film *Good Men, Good Women* itself.[57] Whereas, in the end, *A City of Sadness* concentrated on matters of social situation, at the heart of *Good Men, Good Women* is a broader and deeper consideration of the human moral condition.

Hou Hsiao-hsien's *A City of Sadness* followed the end of martial law in 1987 and was a major political event in Taiwan, contributing to the normalization that had already begun. In *HHH: Portrait of Hou Hsiao-Hsien*, Hou recalls of the filming, "I was aware of the political pressure. It was harsh back then. A slight ideological slip meant trouble. . . ." The film follows the lives of one family's members through the changes from Japanese colonization to the Nationalist takeover, a family that like Taiwan itself included intellectuals, businessmen, mobsters, idealists, and opportunists. The same elements are found in *Good Men, Good Women*, and Hou weaves his two chief thematic interests from these elements and explores the tension between them: Taiwan's distinctive history and its modern fate on the one hand, and Taiwan's gangster underworld on the other. Hou's historical interests center on the question of Taiwanese and "Chinese" identity and the pursuit of social justice for the people of island Taiwan. His fascination with Taiwan's criminal underground mirrors these same questions but from a different angle. Like Faulkner, whose Old South was visibly giving way to a simulacrum of the real thing, and who as a localist loved and recorded for all time its vanishing social diversity from aristocrats to rednecks, former slaves, and sharecroppers, from swashbuckling old colonels and barn burners to New South bankers, Hou Hsiao-hsien's life has spanned Taiwan's transformation from regional isolation into economic dragon, and his cast of characters represents all walks of Taiwanese life, responding to this contested space and time. As told in his early, autobiographical *A Time to Live, A Time to Die* (1985), Hou was born in Meixian, Guangdong province, but in 1948 his family followed his father to the province of Taiwan.[58] The family arrived together with the flood of mainlanders fleeing the Communist revolution and assuming control of provincial politics. While his parents always intended to return, buying only temporary furniture for the household and virtually keeping their bags packed, and his senescent grandmother daily walked off in the direction of the mainland as if she could get there on foot, Hou grew up to cherish his island home. He didn't cross the straits until 1982, attending a film festival in Hong Kong, where he had his first opportunity to watch a mainland film. In the documentary *HHH,* Hou reports on how conscious this made him, for the first time, of the imposition of mainland culture in Taiwan, where the native dialect was banned from use in schools, and talk of the political suppression that accompanied the Nationalist takeover of the island was strictly taboo. "Instantly," he says, "you realized that all the early education has engraved this thing on you [he touches his head]. All your education is education about mainland China." "You're thrilled, as if seeing home for the first time," he says, but when asked, "Are you a Taiwanese or a Chinese director?" he responds, "I'm a Taiwanese director. Culturewise, you can't deny that you are a Chinese. But the political reality, together with the standoff, you cannot deny that you are a Taiwanese. A Taiwanese director."

As described already in *A City of Sadness,* there is nothing new about gangland activity in Taiwan. Just as in Shanghai or Chicago, such pursuits typically emerge among groups divested or excluded from privileged connections, and each disruptive wave of arrivals in Taiwan, first Japanese and later mainland Chinese contingents, promoted new waves of underworld activity among the most recently dispossessed. Despite his late father's intellectual status and administrative standing, Hou Hsiao-hsien testifies in *HHH* that he himself became part of Taipei's prevalent gangster scene in his teens: "I was an enforcer when things arose."

> As a society evolves, it grows multifaceted because of conflicts of interest. They take advantage of construction, public works, outside investments. Then there are smuggling, drugs, aided by advanced transportation and smart communication techniques. Some look outside for opportunities. Everything's connected. During this process, some were killed, either by drugs, or in a gunfight, as my friends have just informed me. My family, both my brother and my sister, thought that I was hopeless. I pawned off a lot of valuables and gambled away my money. I did all that and more. I was very happy when the draft came.

Hou concludes, "I resolved to make a movie while I was doing my military service." He doesn't simply put all this down to youthful experience. "Men today are becoming feminine," he says. "I miss the old macho world, a world of competing mad dogs, fighting for lead positions." Much of this has become the grist for his films, Taiwanese *noir* filled with crime and expiation. More importantly, juxtaposed with the subject of colonial identity, this forms the basis for his films to ask, how does gangsterism differ from ordinary political thuggery and imperial militarism, Taiwan having had its share of each?

Here in Taiwan, the society is still quite primitive. The ever-presence of fierce machismo, it's still pretty primitive. You demonstrate your macho at will, like some wild animals. I am particularly interested in the symbols of machismo. Politics could be fulfilling. It is all about power-countering. Though it could be boring to death. Why? Too calculating; too negative. Organized crime, a macho game. Comparatively romantic and forceful. The primitiveness is still here in Taiwan.[59]

Like *Suzhou River*, *Good Men, Good Women* ends with the death of one of the film's two main female leads and the absorption of her role by the other (by the end of *The Day the Sun Turned Cold*, Guan Jian has similarly subsumed the role of his dead father). These roles define alternative sets of values, and the personal choice of whether or not to pursue some "higher" moral standard lies at the core of each film. Neither film, however, attempts an escape from the "problems of the human heart in conflict with itself," so their inner tensions are accepted and absorbed rather than cinematically and artificially resolved. As a result, the injustices which *Good Men, Good Women* bears witness to lead not to any ideological doctoring—social prescriptions, both Communist and Nationalist, having already outlived their shelf life—but rather to the ironic interrogation of a fundamentally existential inversion: which crimes are worse, those committed in the name of "legitimate" authority or those committed without authorization? Who suffers most, the martyred Chung Hao-Tung or the "merely murdered" Ah Wei? Who is more the victim of her age, the morally committed Chiang Bi-Yu or the morally tortured Liang Ching? Which era offers the more profound corruption, the age of unmitigated ideological warfare or the age of small-scale private warfare that merely fills the moral void? What heights, or depths, might Ah Wei have risen or descended to had he been born at an earlier time? How would Chiang Bi-Yu have handled her fate if born, like Liang Ching, into a world that offered no great political cause? Which of these contrasted but paired couples represent the "good men, good women"?

There are, it must be obvious by now, no answers offered to these questions. Hou Hsiao-hsien's penetrating exposure of political violence dwells with surprising ease side by side with his fascination with private corruption. Liang Ching late in the film not only confesses to taking hush money from her boyfriend's killers, she justifies it. Without it, presumably, she would never have become Liang Ching the actress, playing Chiang Bi-Yu. And, in the very next scene where Liang performs the role of the newly widowed Chiang Bi-Yu grieving by her husband's body, it is *by* this corrupting experience that she is prepared to project such intense yet deeply contained emotion. Can she (or we) really understand, let alone bridge, the moral distance between them? Could Chiang Bi-Yu really have understood Liang Ching any better than Liang understood Chiang Bi-Yu? The inability—or better still, the honest refusal—to cinematically "resolve" such moral questions raises *Good Men, Good Women* to a more universal and fragile level. "Bi-Yu," writes Chung Hao-Tung on the eve of his exe-cution, in a letter read as a voice-over after his death, "don't be afraid and don't grieve for me. . . . Father, Mother, don't grieve. Brothers, sisters, guard your dreams. You have so many talents, you can achieve anything." The sublime tone of Chung's last testament and Chiang Bi-Yu's deeply moving reaction to it deliver the emotional climax of the entire film (*Good Men, Good Women* DVD, Scene 5). At that moment, all the pent-up emotions and restraint of the film, all the decades of pain depicted in it, are released, and yet it is in response to Hao-Tung's own remarkable self-restraint that this takes place. All trace of enmity is set aside in a document—couched in humil-ity (urging Bi-Yu not to "squander" money on his funeral but to worry instead about his child's bad teeth: "I fear it runs in the family") and necessarily disguising in vague terms his socialist aspirations for Taiwan ("guard your dreams . . . you can achieve anything")—which might well remind an American audience of the famous, gentle words of Bartolomeo Vanzetti as he awaited a similar martyrdom.[60]

In the lofty Vanzetti spirit, and much like Faulkner, director Hou Hsiao-hsien leaves himself vulnerable to the charge of being an apologist by refusing to condemn those whom history and fate assigned the task of carrying out evil deeds, often in the name of "good" causes; but for that—for his belief in the moral vulnerability of *every* human heart—his alloyed and imperfect cinematic characters are all the more real and closer to the rest of us. Neither the one-dimensional idealist he might at first sight seem to be nor an authentic cynic, Hou is perhaps best understood as a forgiving fatal-ist, responsive to the never-ending struggle between the dragon and the tiger, a philoso-pher of natural balance in a world of ceaseless conflict. His cinematic "take" is at one and the same time one of sublime spiritual detachment and deeply felt compassion.

In *Suzhou River*, Mudan *might* have been reincarnated as Meimei, but she wasn't; yet the living Meimei *is* reincarnated, figuratively, in the spirit of the deceased Mudan. Liang Ching is similarly "reborn" as a cinematic Chiang Bi-Yu. *Good Men, Good Women*, like *Suzhou River*, can legitimately be regarded as a Chinese ghost story, rolling forward on wheels of karma. Throughout the film, ghosts abound, or are imagined, to prepare for the possibility of Liang Ching's spiritual rebirth. Earlier, when Liang might have borne a child as "a reincarnated Ah Wei" (her words), she didn't (did she abort the pregnancy, after all, or did she give up an infant, like Chiang Bi-Yu?); yet in her final (one-sided) conversation with her anonymous phone caller, she addresses "him" *as if* he were Ah Wei, Ah Wei's tormented spirit, borne of her own betrayal and now tormenting her for it. And his ghost is kept alive by the tormented spirit of her own earlier life as a bar girl. The fax machine has a shamanic function as a continu-ing presence throughout the film, serving as a medium between the specular and the spectral. The strong presence of these spirits remind us that all historical writing is a form of ghost story, and that ghost stories rarely fail to provide a historical moral. Taiwan is full of ghosts; some are political, some personal, and they are often hard to separate and sort out. But the ghost that haunts all Taiwan today is the "one-China policy," first articulated in the Shanghai Communiqué of 1972. This was embraced not just by Maoist China and Nixonian America but by the Nationalist government as well, which maintained the Manchu claim to vast mainland authority (including Mongolia and Tibet) until 1987. Rejected now by the Democratic Progressive Party, which gained control of Taiwan's presidency in the year 2000 and the legislature in 2001, this is one of the ghosts that haunts *Good Men, Good Women*—the ghost of its government's own hubris. Betrayal is essential to most ghost stories, and Taiwan, which has known betrayal well, has every reason to fear that due to this policy and its own past complicity in it, *it too* may someday become a ghost.

For a film director who emphasizes moral choice rather than the meting out of moral judgment, it is appropriate that Hou Hsiao-hsien provides maximum agency to his actors. "I want my actors to be able to understand the concept, to be able to express things in their own way," he says in the film *HHH*. "They think while they perform. Talking is really a spontaneous thing. Sticking to the dialogues sometimes hampers one's performance. Spontaneous responses are powerful and moving. I always follow this rule. No rehearsals. [I] don't want them to know the materials too well." Scriptwriter Chu T'ien-wen, in *HHH*, reiterates this. "There's no rehearsal," she says, "I don't do the script for the director . . . I do it for the crew who need it to prepare sets, to get the actors ready, to set things right. . . . It's a blueprint for the crew." A storyboard such as the ones Hitchcock designed, which maps out each camera action in advance, leaves no room for such spontaneity. Thus Hou Hsiao-hsien's long takes: there are only fifty-seven shots in this 108-minute film (an average of 114 seconds, almost two minutes, per shot).[61]

As in classic Chinese cinema of the 1930s and '40s, which the earlier scenes here strongly evoke, the barely moving camera films a set stage on which the actors are free to roam and interact spontaneously and create their roles with utmost naturalism, and on which the prior, careful setting of the scene must take the place of dramatic camera movement (fig. 81). Hou writes of this, "This type of structure is like our ancient Chinese theater. It simply gives you a scene without much of a clear narrative, unlike Western drama where all the elements must be put in place. Ellipsis and other indirect narrative methods are, ironically, more clear-cut and to the point."[62] He is equally aware of the relation to traditional Chinese painting, saying that

> You don't have to be restrained by the perspective of traditional drama . . . to attain a kind of freedom. This is like a Chinese painter who paints a plum blossom. He doesn't need to paint the whole tree, just a twig, and it would be enough to leave an impression, not only of its fidelity to the subject but also the feelings it conveys. It asks the viewer to use his own powers of imagination, to join

     THE CHINESE HEART IN CONFLICT WITH ITSELF

in the pleasures of looking with the artist, and to embark on the process of interpretation.[63]

"Sometimes," he says, "my actors would leave the frame, but I still won't change my shot, hence you get an empty shot on the screen. Here, I am using a concept from Chinese Painting—'Liu-bai' (literally, 'to leave a whiteness') which means that even after a character has left the frame, or even when you have an unexplained space outside the frame —though it is empty and imagined—the audience must join together with me to complete the shot."[64] While similar in arrangement, then, both to traditional Chinese painting (figs. 81, 76, and 97) and to staged theater or opera, this is not merely "filmed theater," for Chinese theatrical performance is normally tightly scripted and carefully rehearsed. Rather, it is more like a hybrid cross between theater, producing a nearly stationary view of the stage like that seen by a theatrical audience, and the flexibility of cinematic performance (ordinarily facilitated by multiple takes but here by directorial nondirection).

On Hou's "stage," there are "naturalistic" long silences, with characters visibly thinking about what to say before they say it and whole scenes with no word spoken. Gestures and facial expression take the place of camera motion and the film editor's splicing. The role played by a mirror or a photo, the unchanging angle of a view through prison bars into a cell full of young innocents soon to be led to slaughter (fig. 91); the oppressive darkness at noon of a modern apartment that offers no escape from a tormented conscience (fig. 71; *Good Men, Good Women* DVD, Scene 1); the forever-indoors life in urban Taipei as opposed to the outdoors freedom of mainland scenes that suggest the emotional tug of cultural roots (figs. 77 and 95); the painfully slow camera descent from lofty bird's-eye view to painful ground level intimacy at the farewell to a martyr brought down by brutal politics (figs. 99, 89, and 100; *Good Men, Good Women* DVD, Scene 5): all of these images speak more forcefully than words. Like the pattern of Mahler's symphonic adagios, the pace is slow and stately, the plot suppressed, and following upon the discordant tragedies already accumulated and the melancholic mood established in earlier movements, the sounds of suffering are exquisitely sustained before their tearful resolution into a calm benediction and final triumphant notes reassert the standards of human dignity. In the penultimate scene of *Good Men, Good Women* (fig. 100), the resolution comes through martyr Chung Hao-Tung's restrained but touching final words voiced over the tragic image of Chiang Bi-Yu wordlessly succumbing at last to her own long-suppressed emotions. The final scene, previously shown at the outset of the film but with no clear basis for understanding or empathy, is now repeated with a heightened poignancy derived from the spiritual triumph it represents (fig. 80).

With the actors free to improvise and the camera nearly frozen, little else is left to chance. But when the camera tarries somewhere unexpected or begins to move as if *it* were one of the actors, then it is time to wonder what the director has in mind. In

95 *Good Men, Good Women,* Tree-tops

Suzhou River, the single image that recurs throughout the film to "sum it all up" is the flow of the river itself, "a century . . . of stories here and rubbish" in the words of the narrator; a river of life (though one might also put in an argument for the mermaid in the river as the foremost icon of the film). In *Good Men, Good Women,* as in several earlier films by Hou Hsiao-hsien, the iconic equivalent comes outfitted with branches and leaves. On several occasions in the film, the slowly moving camera dwells tellingly on the upper limbs and branches of trees, catching beams of sunlight as they glisten through the leaves (fig. 95), glimpses of spiritual brilliance filtering through to the dappled world down below, reminiscent of a similar sensitivity to the primal forest found in *The World of Apu* or *Rashomon* (the latter based on a short story appropriately entitled "In a Grove"[65]). The filmmaker lingers repeatedly over this image with *some* evident intent in mind, and the image itself lingers long afterwards in the mind's eye. What is it that inspires the director, the cinematographer, and the film editor to attend to such detail in the midst of such a "people film"? Like everything else in *Good Men, Good Women,* there is no single or unambiguous answer but rather an enriching set of possibilities. As a cinematic device, one can trace this back in Hou's films to his *Summer at Grandpa's* (1984). Shiao-ying Shen discusses Hou's "nature shots"[66] (what others have dubbed his "poetics of landscape"), notes his long focus on a tree in *Daughter of the Nile* (1987), and concludes,

      THE CHINESE HEART IN CONFLICT WITH ITSELF

Those who want story action would probably exasperatingly question the right for the existence of such a shot: how does it in any way help forward the action? Exactly, it does *not* forward the action. It *retards* the action. . . . Hou Hsiao-hsien accords such shots a certain duration so that their initial relation to the story action dissipates in the process. They seem to want the viewer to enjoy the sheer play of the event and lose track of one's pursuit of the action. They reveal a desire to not simply mean.[67]

While I agree with the first part of her statement (though there is rarely much "action" to retard anyhow) and would concur that there is a significant and revealing *emptiness* here, this does not imply any simple lack of meaning. Such an image comes with strong associations in China—stronger for being multiple, and for including "emptiness" among them—that are possible to call upon here and that alert us further to the utmost care with which the artist has honed the details of his film. These images, these trees, are major figures in the cast of characters. "Sometimes a cigar is just a cigar"— Freud may or may not have uttered this statement (no written source for it has been found), but one wishes that he had. As a statement about the power of allegorical reference, its force is the reverse of its intent; the cigar *may* be just a cigar, but one cannot hear it expressed in this way, by this man, and think just of cigars. In China, a tree is sometimes just a tree, but no probing of the unconscious is needed to remind people that it could be much more than that.

In a nativist rendering, the image of a huge tree that hovers over Chiang Bi-Yu's arrival in mainland China is a tree of life, embodying sacredness and conveying a larger perspective upon all events that happen within its range. In Ah Cheng's novella *King of the Trees*, set during the political frenzy of the Cultural Revolution, the largest tree in a Yunnanese forest suggests a wisdom that reaches beyond ideology. A huge obstacle in a utilitarian campaign to clear all the forests and plant useful crops,[68] this giant of a tree nonetheless inspires an age-old awe in those commanded to destroy it, calling forth the resident animism that remains deeply rooted in Chinese culture even today.

> Dumbstruck, we approached it slowly and touched the trunk. The bark was not in the least bit tough, and a fingernail was enough to expose the tender green inside. Under our hands it was warm, as if it were a heart beating, so that we wondered *if it had a pulse*.[69]

But Ah Cheng is talking about more than trees, and the vitality of a culture is at stake here:

> The Team Leader looked at it for a moment. "It can't be cut down." We clam-oured for an explanation. The Team Leader slapped at an insect that had landed

96 Fan Kuan, *Travellers among Streams and Mountains,* detail, ca. 1000. National Palace Museum, Taiwan (from Wen Fong, *Possessing the Past*)

97 Muqi, *Gibbons,* ca.1260. Daitokuji, Kyoto (from *Bunjinga suihen* 3)

on his face. "That tree's become a spirit. Anyone who fells it will be in trouble." "What kind of trouble?" we asked. "Death."[70]

When the great tree is finally felled, the local woodsman who with great reluctance helped to bring it down falls ill and never gets up again. Like the slaying of Faulkner's famous bear, this taking brands the culture as one that mistakes obligation for ownership. Ah Cheng's tale ends with an image that conflates tree and man, nature and politics in an allegory of corruption and fate:

> As we went about our work on the mountain, we'd often stop and gaze across: we could see the huge trunk, scarred like a man who'd fallen, and we could also see the patch of white flowers like the white bones exposed in dismembered limbs.[71]

Ironically, perhaps, there is a trajectory here that leads from emptiness, a depletion of natural space, to the reestablishment of that space according to morally resonant order, the tree personifying the scars and bones of the fallen team leader. In this latter vein, the passage quoted in the previous chapter from the Ming-dynasty short story

"Magistrate Teng Settles the Case of Inheritance with Ghostly Cleverness" typifies the metaphoric use of such imagery in a social rhetoric steeped in analogy: "Those who show filial piety to their parents and love and honor whatever their parents love and honor will, for the sake of the parents, extend such feelings to their brothers, *who are like branches on the same tree*. Thus, how can there be any lack of harmony?"[72] Throughout Chinese literature and paintings, for well over a thousand years, references to trees were intended to convey the themes of moral virtue, community, the community of the virtuous, and conversely the forces that drive men together or apart (fig. 96). Coincidentally, or maybe not, the "knots" and "gnarls" on an old tree are written with the same character and pronounced the same as a common word for virtue, *jie*. The grand patriarch of northern Chinese landscape painting, Jing Hao, of the early tenth century, made such trees a staple of his landscapes, loaded his prose and poetry with their symbolic import,[73] and generations of his followers did the same.[74] Deng Chun in 1167 wrote about Jing Hao's follower, Li Cheng, "As for the wintry trees he composed, many are among cliffs and caves, cut off from interiors and completely free. They allude to gentlemen, out of office. As for the remaining trees, their entire lives are (passed) on the level ground. They allude to petty men who hold (official) positions."[75] Trees, like mirrors, became an instrument of moral measure. By extension, as depicted in paintings of life above ground, the branches of the trees were home to the wisest, most harmonious of animals, the mysterious gibbon (fig. 97), which disdains to touch the earth.[76]

Good Men, Good Women brings *all* such references to mind, and note the moments when it does so:

• when Chiang Bi-yu and Chung Hao-Tung first arrive at their mainland destination to serve their cause, where to their dismay they will be shackled and narrowly escape execution;

• when introducing Liang Ching as a hardworking and very pregnant resistance nurse (here an isolated shot with an unmoving camera lasts a full twenty-three seconds) (fig. 95);

• when, during a train ride, Liang Ching first divulges to the audience her receipt of hush money after the murder of Ah Wei;

• and again, when Japanese raiders seize the food reserves of Chiang Bi-Yu's resistance troupe (fig. 90), which incorporates the narration of the couple's return to Taiwan and the loss of their second son.

Punctuated by this unusual cinematic distraction from the matter at hand, these are moments of the most intense companionship and separation, of loyalty and extreme alienation.

Neutral matter to a Western audience but intensely moral for the Chinese, the arboreal image lends its nobility to those who pass under its branches, and perhaps offers

Good Men, Good Women, Disco Dancing

its protection. If the tree suggests the love of native soil, the freedom and dignity of the countryside as opposed to the collective imprisonment of the city, it does not distinguish this soil from that, Taiwan from China. It is especially poignant that these trees are rooted, and filmed, in Hou Hsiao-hsien's own native Guangdong province. The image shown of tree limbs tightly branching, all extending from a single trunk, personifies the family of man in all its complexity, rooted together yet separating in development, all reaching out but tracing separate and often crossed paths. In the film's wordless and most mysterious scene (a critical moment in which music and imagery establish the emotional trajectory for the final climactic scene, which remains ambiguous even to Hou himself[77]), when Liang Ching, her sister, and Tong-Tong dance together, seem both to weep and laugh, and dance again, presumably setting their personal jealousies aside and reconciling in the aftermath of tragedy (fig. 98), do they not look like the branches of a tree, intertwined, with the light streaming down among them? When in the last scenes the camera descends from the upper balcony of Chiang's home, where the daylight pours in through the rails, to the shadowed floor below where the martyred body of Chung Hao-Tung lies beside his grieving widow (figs. 99, 89, and 100; *Good Men, Good Women* DVD Scene 5), are we not descending from the lofty tree tops, with their hope and their wisdom, to the obscured darkness of the grave? Why, the visual rhetoric demands, are we killing one another? In a rare departure from a level encounter with the performers as typically seen by the camera (and by the film audience)—humane and equalizing—the balcony is first seen here from far below (Heaven as seen by man); then the scene below is viewed from the balcony above (man as seen by Heaven, small and pitiable); finally, after the realization of such alternative perspectives, the camera descends, and human norms are restored in a close and emotionally climactic encounter with grief and sublimation. The film's recurrent music, resembling a hymn or anthem, first heard at the first sight of lofty trees as the patriots arrive in China, captures the grief and beauty of the film's humanitarian theme in musical strains that rise and fall, twist and twine like branches. At the film's conclusion, a plaintive wail is added to this Celtic-inspired melody, voicing the bittersweet tragedy—crushing yet transcendent, unleashing emotions so long withheld, culturally and personally suppressed but released at last, and sustaining them throughout the final credits sequence with the sobriety of organ, the purity of flute, and finally with the dignified, funereal hush of muffled drums (*Good Men, Good Women* DVD, Scene 5).

The film's poignant closing imagery requires some expressive formulation, and an aphorism found near the beginning of the epic twelfth-century novel of brotherhood and battle, *The Water-Margin* (Shuihu zhuan), offers one: "Day by day must men grow farther and farther apart or closer and closer together."[78] Hou Hsiao-hsien, fatalist but not nihilist, accepts that men will do both—bond with some, battle with others, no matter what era they live in, each to his own cause, and at any given moment's time who can tell whether his preferred cause is noble and just or not, or how much grief his chosen struggle will bring to others? Hou may not be the best of patriots. Causes, to him, are merely conflicts. He makes a decent Daoist but a peculiar Buddhist, for to him, while karmic merit and debt *may* indeed operate, good fate and bad are not *justly* inherited and deserved. His people may be reincarnations;

99   *Good Men, Good Women*, Balcony

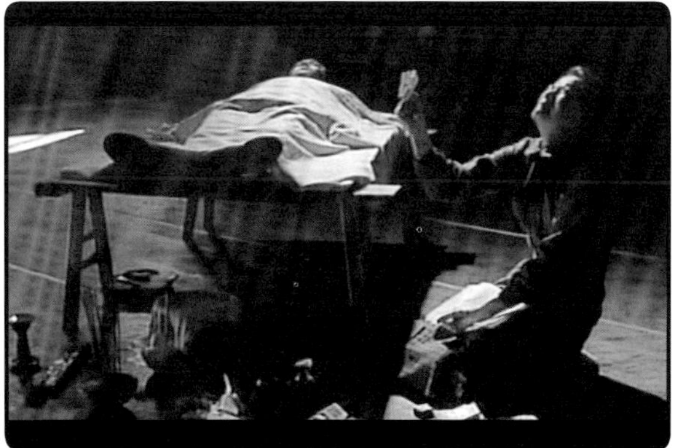

100   *Good Men, Good Women*, Prayers for the Dead

his people may do good things or bad; his people may be idealists or thugs. But is it really possible to pass moral judgment on any one person or generation? In his preceding film, *The Puppetmaster*, Hou showed life itself to be a kind of puppet show, with all the strings attached, political, social, and psychological. Here, in *Good Men, Good Women*, living in the clutches of fate, people are arbitrarily shaped by events of the moment, by what history has to offer, and none is less worthy of pity and compassion than any other, no more than one tree branch is less deserving of space and water and sunlight than any other. Rather, they are *all* good men and good women.

Introduction

Epigraphs: Shi Nai'an (attributed), *The Water-Margin* (Shuihu zhuan), trans. by Pearl Buck as *All Men Are Brothers* (New York: Grosset and Dunlap/John Day, 1937), 19. William Faulkner, *Essays, Speeches, and Public Letters*, ed. James B. Meriwether (New York: Random House, 1966), 119–20.

1. *Suzhou River* was awarded the grand prize at the Paris Film Festival, and Zhou Xun (performing in two separate roles, both as an adult and as a young adolescent) was honored as best actress; a special award was presented at the Rotterdam Festival to writer-director Lou Ye, citing his "experimentation in narrative forms and successful evocation of loss and wonder in the modern city." *The Day the Sun Turned Cold* won the best film award at the Tokyo Film Festival, and Yim Ho received the prize for best director. *Good Men, Good Women* won the award for best film at the Hawaii International Film Festival and a special achievement award at the Singapore Film Festival. Director Hou Hsiao-hsien received Taiwan's Golden Horse award, and Chu T'ien-wen won the Golden Horse award for best adapted screenplay.

2. For example, see Rey Chow, *Primitive Passions: Visuality, Sexuality, Ethnography, and Contemporary Chinese Cinema* (New York: Columbia University Press, 1995), 88, 95; Paul Clark, "The Sinification of Cinema: The Foreignness of Film in China," in *Cinema and Cultural Identity: Reflections on Films from Japan, India, and China*, ed. Wimal Dissanayake (Lanham, Md.: University Press of America, 1988), 175–84.

3. Jerome Silbergeld, *China into Film: Frames of Reference in Contemporary Chinese Cinema* (London: Reaktion Books, 1999), 9–11; Lothar Ledderose, *Ten Thousand Things: Module and Mass Production in Chinese Art* (Princeton: Princeton University Press, 2000).

4. The first peep-show film was shown in a Shanghai teahouse in 1896. Film was first shown publicly in Beijing in 1902. In Hong Kong, the first comedies were made in 1909, and a full-length Cantonese opera was performed on film in 1913.

5. In these two cases, Frank Borzage's *Street Angel* (1937) and Vittorio De Sica's *Bicycle Thief* (1948), respectively. For notes on the evolution of *Street Angel* from London play to American film to Chinese film, see Silbergeld, *China into Film*, 317, n. 8, and 328, n. 53.

6. Gabriel García Márquez's *One Hundred Years of Solitude* is the other work cited by Mo Yan. Faulkner and García Márquez are typically cited as the two most influential foreign writers in China today. The English Department of Beijing University hosted a four-day Faulkner international conference in November 1997, the centennial of his birth.

7. Silbergeld, *China into Film*, 100–105, compares the cinematic devices used in *Farewell My Concubine* with the climactic scenes of *The Godfather*. On John Woo's film techniques, see David Bordwell, *Planet Hong Kong: Popular Cinema and the Art of Entertainment* (Cambridge: Harvard University Press, 2000), 98–114.

8. Sheldon Lu, "Historical Introduction: Chinese Cinemas (1896–1996) and Transnational Film Studies," in *Transnational Chinese Cinemas: Identity, Nationhood, Gender*, ed. Sheldon Lu (Honolulu: University of Hawai'i Press, 1997), 25 (my italics).

9. On melodrama in Chinese cinema, see the essays by Ma Ning, William Rothman, Eugene Wang, and Ann Kaplan in Wimal Dissanayake, *Melodrama and Asian Cinema* (New York:

Cambridge University Press, 1993); Paul Pickowicz, "Melodramatic Representation and the 'May Fourth' Tradition of Chinese Cinema," in *From May Fourth to June Fourth: Fiction and Film in Twentieth-Century China*, ed. Ellen Widmer and David Der-wei Wang (Cambridge: Harvard University Press, 1993), 295–326; Nick Browne, "Society and Objectivity: On the Political Economy of Chinese Melodrama," in *New Chinese Cinemas: Forms, Identities, Politics*, ed. Nick Browne et al. (New York: Cambridge University Press, 1994), 40–41; and Silbergeld, *China into Film*, chaps. 5 ("The Force of Labels: Melodrama in the Postmodern Era") and 6 ("The Children of Melodrama: No-drama, Pseudo-drama, Melodramatic Masquerade and Deconstruction Drama").

10. One might note the increasing frequency of PRC films that examine these psychological dimensions, such as *Army Nurse* (director Hu Mei, 1985), *Transmigration* (Samsara, director Huang Jianxin, 1988), *Black Snow* (director Xie Fei, 1990), *Temptress Moon* (director Chen Kaige, 1996), *Frozen* (Jidu hanleng, director Wang Xiaoshuai, 1996), *East Palace*, *West Palace* (director Zhang Yuan, 1997), as well as Hong Kong and Taiwan films, such as Stanley Kwan's *Rouge* (1987) and *Red Rose*, *White Rose* (1994), Wong Kar-Wai's *Happy Together* (1997) and *In the Mood for Love* (2000), Yang Dechang's (Edward Yang's) *The Terrorizer* (1986) and *Yi Yi* (2000), and Tsai Ming-liang's film sequence including *Rebels of the Neon God* (1992) and *The River* (1997).

But just as there is an obvious difference between a neurotic patient and an analyst, one must differentiate between a film which provides interesting case material and one which establishes its own psychoanalytic structure or at least presents a structured entry into such a reading within the film itself. This can be typified by the contrast between *Hibiscus Town* (1986) and *Army Nurse*. Gu Hua's novel, *A Small Town Called Hibiscus* (Beijing: Panda Books, 1983), presents a clear case of sexual self-loathing sublimated into political fanaticism, but Xie Jin's cinematic adaptation of this virtually erases this psychological dimension; *Army Nurse*, on the other hand, with the aid of an inner narrative, focuses clearly on the channeling of sexual energy into the service of the state and the high price paid by the individual for the suppression of personality and sexual desire (see Silbergeld, *China into Film*, 214–17 and 156 ff.). Shuqin Cui has provided a Lacanian reading of Zhang Yimou's *Judou* (1989), but he doesn't claim that the film itself embraces Lacanian principles; see Cui, "Gendered Perspective: The Construction and Representation of Subjectivity and Sexuality in *Ju Dou*," in *Transnational Chinese Cinemas*, ed. Lu, 303–29. In a similar way, David Ing has linked Lacanian theory with patriarchal order in Hong Kong in "Love at Last Site: Waiting for Oedipus in Stanley Kwan's *Rouge*," *Camera Obscura* 32 (1993–94): 75–101. Yingjin Zhang provides an extensive critical response to psychoanalytic readings by Ann Kaplan and Chris Berry; see Yingjin Zhang, *Screening China: Critical Interventions, Cinematic Transformations, and the Transnational Imaginary in Contemporary Chinese Cinema* (Ann Arbor: University of Michigan Center for Chinese Studies, 2002), 120–26 and 133 ff.; E. Ann Kaplan, "Problematizing Cross-Cultural Analysis: The Case of Women in the Recent Chinese Cinema," *Wide Angle* 11, no. 2 (1989): 40–50, reprinted in *Perspectives on Chinese Cinema*, 2nd ed., ed. Chris Berry (London: British Film Institute, 1991), 141–54; E. Ann Kaplan, "Reading Formations and Chen Kaige's *Farewell My Concubine*," in *Transnational Chinese Cinemas*, ed. Lu, 265–75; and Chris Berry, "The Sublimitive Text: Sex and Revolution in *Big Road*," *East-West Film Journal* 2, no. 2 (1988): 66–86.

11. Zhang Junxiang, "Essay Done in Film Terms," in *Chinese Film Theory: A Guide to the New Era*, ed. George Semsel, Xiao Hong, and Hou Jianping (New York: Praeger, 1990), 29; see Silbergeld, *China into Film*, 190–91.

12. For Shanghai in a cinematic context, see Yingjin Zhang, ed., *Cinema and Urban Culture in Shanghai, 1922–1943* (Stanford: Stanford University Press, 1999), especially articles by

Yingjin Zhang, "Prostitution and Urban Imagination: Negotiating the Public and the Private in Chinese Films of the 1930s," 160–80; Michael Chang, "The Good, the Bad, and the Beautiful: Movie Actresses and Public Discourse in Shanghai, 1920s–1930s," 128–59; and Andrew Field, "Selling Souls in Sin City: Shanghai Singing and Dancing Hostesses in Print, Film and Politics, 1920–1949," 99–127, as well as the extensive bibliography on 319–40. See also Leo Lee, *Shanghai Modern: The Flowering of a New Urban Culture in China, 1930* (Cambridge: Harvard University Press, 1999), especially chap. 3, "The Urban Milieu of Shanghai Cinema"; and Elizabeth Perry and Li Xun, *Proletarian Power: Shanghai in the Cultural Revolution* (Boulder: Westview Press, 1997).

13. Pamela Yatsko, *New Shanghai: The Rocky Rebirth of China's Legendary City* (New York: John Wiley and Sons, 2001).

14. Cf. Richard Levy, "Corruption in Popular Culture," in *Popular China: Unofficial Culture in a Globalizing Society*, ed. Perry Link et al. (Lanham, Md.: Rowman and Littlefield, 2002), 39–56.

15. For an overview of how this has played out in academic literature, see Yingjin Zhang, *Screening China*, especially chaps. 2, 3, 4.

16. Rick Moody, *The Ice Storm* (New York: Warner Books, 1994).

17. A study is needed which compares Chinese filmmakers, artists, and writers working domestically with those working outside of Chinese-speaking territory.

18. See Eugene Wang, "What Do Trigrams Have to Do with Buddhas? The Northern Liang Stupas as a Hybrid Spatial Model," *Res* 35 (spring 1999): 70–91.

19. If these films represent just the beginning of such a list, I would quickly add others, such as Tian Zhuangzhuang's *Horse Thief* (1985); Yang Dechang's (Edward Yang's) *The Terrorizer* (1986) and *Confucian Confusion* (1994); Huang Jianxin's *Transmigration* (Samsara, 1988); Tsai Ming-liang's *Rebels of the Neon God* (1992); *Vive l'Amour* (1994), and *The River* (1997); Zhang Yuan's *Beijing Bastards* (1993) and *East Palace, West Palace* (1997); Wong Kar-Wai's *Ashes of Time* (1994), *Chungking Express* (1994), *Fallen Angels* (1995), and *Happy Together* (1997); Jiang Wen's *In the Heat of the Sun* (1994) and *Devils on the Doorstep* (2000); Wang Xiaoshuai's *Frozen* (1996); and Jia Zhangke's *Xiao Wu* (1997) and *Platform* (2000).

20. A decade ago, Chiao Hsiung-Ping wrote cogently of the differences then perceived between Hong Kong and Taiwan film, and they indeed have distinctive histories and trajectories; see Chiao, "The Distinct Taiwanese and Hong Kong Cinemas," in *Perspectives on Chinese Cinema*, ed. Berry, 155–65. But Hong Kong, Taiwan, and PRC film have shared characteristics as well; Jenny Kwok Wah Lau, in the same volume, attempts to define some of those characteristics; see Lau, "A Cultural Interpretation of the Popular Cinema of China and Hong Kong," ibid., 166–74. See also Esther Yau, "Border Crossing: Mainland China's Presence in Hong Kong Cinema," in *New Chinese Cinemas*, ed. Browne et al., 180–201.

21. See chap. 3, p. 100, and DVD *Good Men, Good Women,* Scene 5: The Deaths of Chung Hao-Tung and Chiang Bi-Yu.

22. See chap. 1, n. 49. Fourteen months after the inaugural, seeking international sympathy for its 2008 Olympic bid, the Chinese government lifted its travel ban on A-Mei. See Hannah Beech, "Both Sides Now": www.time.com/time/asia/features/heroes/amei.htm www.geocities.com/purelyamei

23. See Britta Erickson, "Changing Places, Changing Meanings: Chinese Contemporary Art in a Global Environment," in Chen Pao-chen et al., *Quyu yu gangluo: jin qiannianlai Zhongguo meishu shi yanjiu* (Regionality and networking: studies in Chinese art history of the last millennium) (Taipei: National Taiwan University Research Program in Art History), 727–48.

24. Mao Tse-tung, *Talks at the Yenan Forum on Literature and Art* (Beijing: Foreign Languages Press, 1976), 4 (my italics).

25. See Silbergeld, *China into Film*, chap. 3, "A Farewell to Arts: Allegory Goes to the Movies."

26. Vernon Louis Parrington, *Main Currents in American Thought: An Interpretation of American Literature from the Beginnings to 1920* (New York: Harcourt, Brace and Company, 1927), iii.

27. See, however, the essays by Ni Zhen, Hao Dazheng, Jenny Kwok Wah Lau, and Chris Berry and Mary Ann Farquhar in Linda Ehrlich and David Desser, eds., *Cinematic Landscapes: Observations on the Visual Arts and Cinema of China and Japan* (Austin: University of Texas Press, 1994); Ma Ning, "Spatiality and Subjectivity in Xie Jin's Film Melodrama of the New Period," in *New Chinese Cinemas*, ed. Browne et al., 15–39 (which I find more interesting than convincing); also Silbergeld, *China into Film*.

28. Ang Lee, preface to James Schamus, *The Ice Storm: The Shooting Script* (New York: Newmarket Press, 1997), vii.

29. Silbergeld, *China into Film*, 328, n. 67. See my comparison there of a frequently published publicity photo from the film *Army Nurse* with an actual film frame of the "real thing" (figs. 144 and 145, discussed on 164–65).

1. Hitchcock with a Chinese Face: *Suzhou River*

Epigraphs: Slavoj Žižek, *Enjoy Your Symptom! Jacques Lacan in Hollywood and Out*, rev. ed. (New York: Routledge, 2001), 149.

1. As noted in the introduction, the film's subtitles give "Moudan" for Mudan ("Peony"), "Mardar" for Mada, and "Xia-ho" for Xiao Hong ("Little Red"), which threatens to obscure their significance. The name Mudan calls to mind the unconstrained sixteen-year-old romantic Du Liniang from the famous play *The Peony Pavilion* (Mudan Ting). An ancient tale given theatrical form in the late sixteenth century by Tang Xianzu, Du falls in love with her vision of a man and dies of longing for him, but her dream-lover later appears as an actual figure and brings her back to life. See Cyril Birch, trans., *The Peony Pavilion* (Bloomington: Indiana University Press, 1980). The *mudan*, or tree peony, was traditionally associated with aristocratic beauty, which lends the neglected child Mudan a Cinderella-like quality as much for her romantic faith as for her outward appearance. The name Meimei, on the other hand, focuses on an apparent "beauty" whose inner virtues will have to be discovered and developed by the lovely Meimei herself. Mada (literally, "horse arrives") seems an appropriate name for a longed-for male lover and courier whose definitive role in the film is to convey Mudan's inner qualities to Meimei. Red seems a fitting name for Xiao Hong as a traditional label associated with sex and corruption, especially given her bloody demise. One cannot help but think of a contrast with the famous Xiao Hong of Yuan Muzhi's film classic *Street Angel* (1937), a young woman of virtue, unspoiled despite the horrible corruption that surrounds her and envelopes the Shanghai of her day.

2. In 1967, François Truffaut's first edition of *Hitchcock* described him as "until now . . . grossly underrated"; by the time of his second edition, 1983, Truffaut began his introduction with the statement, "Nowadays, the work of Alfred Hitchcock is admired all over the world." François Truffaut, *Hitchcock*, rev. ed. (New York: Simon and Schuster/Touchstone, 1985), 20, 11. Hitchcock was ranked the second-best director of all time in *Sight and Sound*'s 2002 poll of leading critics, fifth in their directors' poll: www.bfi.org.uk/sightandsound/topten/poll/critics.html

In academic writing, see, for example, the role played by Hitchcock's films in Laura Mulvey's influential article, "Visual Pleasure and Narrative Cinema," *Screen* 16, no. 5 (autumn 1975): 6–18. University Microfilms currently lists twenty-three American dissertations with Hitchcock in the title.

3. Truffaut, *Hitchcock*, 19–20, offers an extensive list of major filmmakers and films he considers to have been influenced by Hitchcock. *Vertigo* was rated the second "greatest film of all time" in *Sight and Sound*'s 2002 poll of critics, sixth in their directors' poll: www.bfi.org.uk/sightandsound/topten/poll/critics-directors.html The American Film Institute's poll of more than fifteen hundred filmmakers, historians, scholars, and critics rated *Psycho*, *Rear Window*, and *Vertigo* the eighteenth, forty-second, and sixty-first best American films of all time, respectively: www.afi.com

4. Born in Shanghai, Lou graduated from the Beijing Film Academy in 1994. He lists John Cassavettes, Michelangelo Antonioni, and Federico Fellini as major influences.

5. Lou Ye's first film, *Weekend Lover* (Zhoumo qingren, 1995), was his Beijing Film Academy graduation film and winner of the Rainer Werner Fassbinder award for best director at the Mannheim-Heidelberg Film Festival. A film for television followed, entitled *Don't Be Young* (1995). Lou produced a television series, "Super City," in 1998. For "Super City," reportedly the first digital film project in China, he invited ten members of his Beijing Film Academy graduating class to direct forty-seven-minute Shanghai-based episodes. *Suzhou River* grew out of Lou's own planned two-part contribution to this series, *The Rushing City* (Benpao de chengshi). Huang Shixian reports that only six titles were completed before the funding ran out; see Huang, "Zhongguo 'hunian,'" in *Dangdai Zhongguo dianying: 1998* (Taipei: Shibao wenhua, 1999), 162–65. With the help of German producer Philippe Bober, Lou's project was rescued and filmed on 16 mm film (his first two films were made on 35 mm film stock). "Interview with Brock Norman Brock and Placidus Schelbert," undated, distributed by Strand Releasing; also, no identified author, interview with Lou Ye: www.filmex.net/archives2000/interview/09futarino-e.htm

6. Zhou Xun's (b. 1967) first major role was in *The Emperor and the Assassin* (directed by Chen Kaige, 1999). She has subsequently performed in Wang Xiaoshuai's *Beijing Bicycle* (2001); Fruit Chan's *Hollywood Hong-Kong* (2001); *A Pinwheel Without Wind*, for which she won the prestigious Hundred Flowers Award (2002) for best actress; and *Little Chinese Seamstress* (directed by Dai Sijie, 2002).

7. See Wen Fong, "The Problem of Forgeries in Chinese Painting," *Artibus Asiae* 25 (1962): 95–119; Marilyn Fu [Wong-Gleysteen] and Shen Fu, *Studies in Connoisseurship: Chinese Paintings from the Arthur M. Sackler Collection in New York and Princeton* (Princeton: Princeton University Press, 1973), 16–34.

8. William Arnold, *Seattle Post-Intelligencer*, March 2, 2001, in review of *Suzhou River*'s showing at the Seattle International Film Festival.

9. Slavoj Žižek, *Looking Awry: An Introduction to Jacques Lacan through Popular Culture* (Cambridge, Mass.: MIT Press, 1991), 79.

10. Among numerous works on *Vertigo*, see Donald Spoto, *The Art of Alfred Hitchcock: Fifty Years of His Motion Pictures*, 2nd ed. (New York: Anchor/Doubleday, 1992), 263–99; Dan Auiler, *Vertigo: The Making of a Hitchcock Classic* (New York: St. Martin's Press, 1998); Emanuel Berman, "Hitchcock's *Vertigo:* The Collapse of a Rescue Fantasy," in *Psychoanalysis and Film*, ed. Glen Gabbard (London: Karnac, 2001), 29–62; Charles Barr, *Vertigo* (London: British Film Institute, 2002).

11. In a closing section cut from the original release of *Vertigo* but still available on video, Scottie returns to his former girlfriend, Midge, in a catatonic state of depression.

12. Hitchcock once explained a MacGuffin as such: "It might be a Scottish name, taken from a story about two men in a train. One man asks, 'What's that package up there in the baggage rack?' And the other answers, 'Oh, that's a MacGuffin.' The first one asks, 'What's a Mac-Guffin?' 'Well,' the other man says, 'it's an apparatus for trapping lions in the Scottish Highlands.' The first man says, 'But there are no lions in the Scottish Highlands,' and the other one answers, 'Well then, that's no MacGuffin!' So you see that a MacGuffin is actually nothing at all." Truffaut, *Hitchcock*, 138.

13. The son of a theater director, Jia Hongsheng graduated from the Central Academy of Drama in 1989 and performed on stage in Beijing as the gay prisoner Luis in *Kiss of the Spider Woman*, directed by Zhang Yang. He became popular through a number of gangster films and television appearances. He played in *Good Morning, Beijing* (Beijing, Ni zao; directed by Zhang Nuanxin, 1991), then starred in Lou Ye's first film, *Weekend Lover* (1995) and afterwards in Wang Xiaoshuai's *Frozen* (1996) as a performance artist whose final performance is a suicide. At about this time, Jia became addicted to heroin, withdrew from acting, and was eventually arrested and committed to a state-run mental hospital. His personal saga has been dramatized in the film *Quitting* (Zuotian—literally, "Yesterday"; 2001) by his friend Zhang Yang, director of the internationally successful *Shower*. In *Quitting*, Jia plays himself, along with the other members of his family and even his fellow hospital-ward members, and the film is unusual for its depiction (albeit, notably benign) of a Chinese mental institution. Lou Ye's *Suzhou River* provided the occasion for Jia's cinematic comeback, and its characterization of Mada is very much shaped by Jia's own emotional peculiarities. *Quitting*, however, does not refer to *Suzhou River* and Jia's post-rehabilitation activities. *Quitting* and Zhang Yang won the Golden Swing prize for best film at the Bangkok Film Festival, the FIPRESCI Award ("for its combination of documentary and dramatic methods") at the Stockholm Film Festival, and the NETPAC award at the Venice Film Festival, while Jia Hongsheng won the award for best actor at the Singapore International Film Festival.

14. Dennis Lim, "Lou Ye's Generation Next," *Village Voice*, November 14, 2000, 140.

15. In Jonah Greenberg,"Voyeur Eyes Only: Lou Ye's Variations on Romance," *Virtual China*, 1999: www.virtualchina.com

16. Similarly, screenwriter Joseph Stefano was undergoing psychoanalysis while writing *Psycho* and claimed to have brought this experience directly into play.

17. As indicated in n. 11 above, a major exception to this would have been *Vertigo*'s original ending, but this was jettisoned.

18. Cf. Slavoj Žižek, "Why Does the Phallus Appear?" in Žižek, *Enjoy Your Symptom!* 117–20.

19. In Glen Gabbard and Krin Gabbard, *Psychiatry and the Cinema*, 2nd ed. (Washington, D.C.: American Psychiatric Press, 1999), xvi.

20. Irving Schneider, in Gabbard and Gabbard, *Psychiatry and the Cinema*, xv.

21. Martin Whyte, review of Richard H. Solomon, *Mao's Revolution and the Chinese Political Culture*, in *American Journal of Sociology* 79, no. 5 (March 1974): 1355.

22. See, for example, Margery Wolf's classic article, "Child Training and the Chinese Family," in *Family and Kinship in Chinese Society*, ed. Maurice Friedman (Stanford: Stanford University Press, 1970), 37–62; and Hugh Baker, *Chinese Family and Kinship* (New York: Columbia University Press, 1979).

23. Yuejin [Eugene] Wang, "*Red Sorghum*: Mixing Memory and Desire," in *Perspectives on Chinese Cinema*, ed. Berry, 83.

24. See Louise Edwards, *Men and Women in Qing China: Gender in The Red Chamber Dream* (Honolulu: University of Hawai'i Press, 1994), particularly chap. 3, "Gender Imperatives: Jia

Baoyu's Bisexuality"; chap. 4, "Young Women and Prescriptions of Purity"; and chap. 7, "Jia Family Women: Unrestrained 'Indulgent Mothers.'" On *Family* in film, see Silbergeld, *China into Film*.

25. Wolf, "Child Training and the Chinese Family," 61.

26. At a symposium entitled "Non-Economic Aspects of China's Economic Reforms" (Harvard University, September 1996), Arthur Kleinman presented current data to the effect that 42 percent of all the world's suicides occur in China (four times the per capita rate of the United States); that unlike most nations, China's suicides are predominantly rural (five to seven times greater than the urban suicide rate); and that only in China do more women than men commit suicide.

27. For Freud's view of the triangulated sexual relationship between Hamlet, his mother, and his uncle, and the psychosexual basis of his hesitancy, see chap. 2, n. 13. See also Sigmund Freud, *The Interpretation of Dreams*, trans. A. A. Brill, in *The Basic Writings of Sigmund Freud* (New York: Random House, 1938; originally published 1900), 309–11; Freud, "Dostoevsky and Parricide," trans. D. F. Tait, in *Standard Edition of the Collected Psychological Works of Sigmund Freud*, ed. James Strachey (London: Hogarth Press, 1953–74; originally published as a book preface, 1928); reprinted in *Dostoevsky: A Collection of Critical Essays*, ed. René Wellek (Englewood Cliffs, N.J.: Prentice-Hall, Inc., 1962), 107.

28. See Silbergeld, *China into Film*, 120–31, for a discussion of the Fifth Generation town-to-city film *The Story of Qiu Ju* (1992), which helped introduce a blurring of cinematic fiction and documentary style, along with films like Xie Fei's *Black Snow* (1990, cinematography by Xiao Feng). In *The Story of Qiu Ju*, however, the camera was hidden in trucks and on rooftops, whereas here it has become a virtual participant in the scene with a recognized role in the narrative. The hand-held camera was popularized in Chinese-language films by the Australian cinematographer Christopher Doyle (*That Day on the Beach*, Taiwan, 1983; *Ashes of Time*, Hong Kong, 1994; *Chungking Express*, Hong Kong, 1994; *Red Rose, White Rose*, Hong Kong, 1994; *Fallen Angels*, 1995; *Temptress Moon*, People's Republic, 1996; *Happy Together*, Hong Kong, 1997; *In the Mood for Love*, Hong Kong, 2000) and has become increasingly popular in recent post–Fifth Generation films like Jia Zhangke's *Xiao Wu* (1997, cinematography by Xu Liwei) and Jiang Wen's *Devils on the Doorstep* (2000, cinematography by Gu Changwei).

29. Truffaut, *Hitchcock*, 248.

30. See the *Shan hai jing* for the Di people, descendants of the Emperor Yan, who have "human faces, fish bodies and no legs"; and the early nineteenth-century illustrated edition of Kuo Po's (276–324) "eulogies," the *Shan hai tu zan*, "The progeny of Emperor Yen / Produced the Di People, who / After dying, can revive; / On their bodies are scales and / Clouds and rain hold them up, as / They swim in the River of Heaven [the Milky Way]." Hsiao-Cheng Cheng et al., trans., *Shan Hai Ching: Legendary Geography and Wonders of Ancient China* (Taipei: National Institute for Compilation and Translation, 1985), 180, 362.

31. In Jonathan Rosenbaum, "The World Is Watching," *Chicago Reader*, 2001: www.chireader.com

32. Hans Christian Andersen, "The Little Mermaid," in *Tales and Stories by Hans Christian Andersen*, trans. Pat Conroy and Sven Rossel (Seattle: University of Washington Press, 1980), 34–58.

33. Silbergeld, *China into Film*, chap. 1. See also the various entries indexed under "drowning and suicide" in this volume.

34. See, for example, *The Girl from Hunan* (directed by Xie Fei, 1985).

35. For example, *Woman from the Lake of Scented Souls* (directed by Xie Fei, 1992) and Su

Tong's novella *Raise the Red Lantern*, trans. Michael Duke (New York: William Morrow, 1993).

36. See n. 26 above. On the continuing gender inequality of contemporary China, see Paul Pickowicz and Liping Wang, "Village Voices, Urban Activists: Women, Violence, and Gender Inequality in Rural China," in *Popular China*, ed. Link et al., 56–87.

37. Silbergeld, *China into Film*, chaps. 1 ("Drowning on Dry Land") and 4 ("The Veil of Tradition: Victims, Warriors, and the Female Analogy").

38. In recent decades, female suicide by submergence has been largely supplanted by ingestion of liquid pesticides, particularly among rural women.

39. Cao Zhi [Ts'ao Chih], "The Goddess of the Luo," in *Chinese Rhyme-Prose: Poems from the Chinese in Fu Form from the Han and Six Dynasties Periods*, trans. David Hawkes (New York: Columbia University Press, 1971), 56–57.

40. The quintessential such tale, no doubt, is Tao Yuanming's (365–427) immortal "Peach Blossom Spring," where the romance is personified not by a beautiful female but rather an entire Edenesque village lost in timelessness. The reintroduction of female beauty into such a site occurs in Zhao Cangyun's illustrated tale, *Liu Chen and Ruan Zhao in the Tiantai Mountains;* see Maxwell Hearn's essay in Maxwell Hearn and Wen Fong, *Along the Riverbank: Chinese Paintings from the C. C. Wang Family Collections* (New York: Metropolitan Museum of Art, 1999), 80–92.

41. The English subtitles translate the expression slightly differently with each iteration: "If I leave you . . ." and "If I left you . . ." In fact, the text and voice are the same, played twice.

42. Silbergeld, *China into Film*, 116–19.

43. Perry Link and Kate Zhou, "Shunkouliu: Popular Satirical Sayings and Popular Thought," in *Popular China*, ed. Link et al., 89–109.

44. Interview in Levy, "Corruption in Popular Culture," 46.

45. Ibid., 49.

46. Cf. Robert Porfiro, "No Way Out: Existential Motifs in the *Film Noir*," in *Film Noir Reader*, ed. Alain Silver and James Ursini (New York: Limelight Editions, 1996), 77–93.

47. Since 1989, for example, activities in Beijing's Tian'an Men Square have been thoroughly monitored by stationary cameras, which everyone is fully aware of and which people can even be seen walking beneath and waving to. On the related phenomenon of arts censorship, see n. 51 below.

48. Cf. David King, *The Commissar Vanishes: The Falsification of Photographs and Art in Stalin's Russia* (New York: Metropolitan Books/Henry Holt and Company, 1997). Perhaps a similar volume will one day document this aspect of photographic history in China.

49. The film's credits do not mention the new actress introduced here—as if to maintain this ambiguity—or the song title and A-Mei. Only the first four lines are translated in the English subtitles. The remainder is my translation. The lyrics are:

> Love is a city without night, but memories are like stars,
> Hot tears growing hotter as feelings grow cold.
> When your heart is changing, the more you think the more it hurts
> You sit up listlessly until dawn, till the sun takes the place of the lights in your room.
> Thoughts: if it looks like things are coming to an end, why think about the pain?
> Hurt: if you're willing to act grown up about it, why fear the hurt of parting?
> Letting go means ready to admit it's a thing gone wrong,
> That you shouldn't be afraid to go free
> You've got your right to go, I've got my right to a happy parting
> Letting go means knowing to wipe away old tears, look ahead,

Find new directions toward the future

This world is huge, I can always make a dream come true.

Thoughts: if it looks like things are coming to an end, why think about the pain?

Hurt: if you're willing to act grown up about it, why fear the hurt of parting?

Letting go means ready to admit it's a thing gone wrong,

That you shouldn't be afraid to go free

You've got your right to go, I've got my right to a happy parting

In my heart I've got something bolder to yearn for,

Don't want my lover worrying about me anymore.

50. Zhuangzi's famous passage on this reads, "Call in your knowledge, unify your bearing, and the spirits will come to dwell with you. Virtue will be your beauty, the Way will be your home, and, *stupid* as a newborn calf, you will not try to find out the reason why." Burton Watson, trans., *The Complete Works of Chuang Tzu* (New York: Columbia University Press, 1970), 131 (italics added).

51. The Film Bureau is an agency of the government's State Administration for Radio, Film, and Television (SARFT), while the Film Distribution Corporation is an arm of the Communist Party's Propaganda Department. In this regard, it is generally even more difficult to get a film officially distributed than it is to get one made. On film censorship, see Mayfair Yang, "Of Gender, State, Censorship, and Overseas Capital: An Interview with Chinese Director Zhang Yimou," *Public Culture* 5 (1993): 297–313, reprinted in *Zhang Yimou: Interviews*, ed. Frances Gateward (Jackson: University of Mississippi Press, 2001), 34–49. On film censorship in earlier decades, see Zhiwei Xiao, "Anti-Imperialism and Film Censorship during the Nanjing Decade, 1927–1937," in *Transnational Chinese Cinemas*, ed. Lu, 35–57; Zhiwei Xiao, "Constructing a New National Culture: Film Censorship and the Issues of Cantonese Dialect, Superstition, and Sex in the Nanjing Decade," in *Cinema and Urban Culture in Shanghai*, ed. Yingjin Zhang, 183–99. For state censorship in the visual arts more broadly, see Jerome Silbergeld with Gong Jisui, *Contradictions: Artistic Life, the Socialist State, and the Chinese Painter Li Huasheng* (Seattle and London: University of Washington Press, 1993). For the state's censorial role in traditional times, see Kent Guy, *The Emperor's Four Treasuries: Scholars and the State in the Late Ch'ien-lung Era* (Cambridge: Council on East Asian Studies, Harvard University, 1987).

52. See n. 5 above.

53. In his interview with Jonah Greenberg, Lou notes that his previous film, *Weekend Lover* (1995), remained in the censor's hands for two years before release. The larger question is what cuts or other changes might be required of the original in order to gain Chinese authorization.

54. My analysis and interpretation of these films were purposely undertaken without direct input from these filmmakers. However, after this text was completed and edited, I received the following response from *Suzhou River*'s director, Lou Ye: "In shooting, it was my assistant director who played the role of 'I' [the narrator]. It was I who dubbed the voice, which naturally included the off-screen voice [the voice-over]. [This was because] when shooting, I mostly had to stay next to my cameraman watching the filming through a small monitor, keeping open a communications channel with him at all times. In the film, Mada was really a reflected image (of myself) 'in a mirror.' It felt like I was watching a stranger (Mada) in a mirror, and when he (Mada) and I meet eye-to-eye (through the camera) then I suddenly sense that that stranger in the mirror is the same as myself. Although (I) don't appear in the film, just a hand or a few other bits or a few shadows, presentation of the feelings of this character [Mada, myself] is achieved completely through my observation of things, including the young girl who is seen

singing a sorrowful song for (me)." Personal communication, October 7, 2003 (parentheses here are Lou Ye's own).

2. Oedipus Comes to Hong Kong: *The Day the Sun Turned Cold*

Epigraphs: Sigmund Freud, *The Interpretation of Dreams*, in *The Basic Writings of Sigmund Freud*, trans. A. A. Brill (New York: Random House, 1938; originally published 1900), 307–8; Sigmund Freud, "Dostoevsky and Parricide," trans. D. F. Tait. In *Standard Edition of the Collected Psychological Works of Sigmund Freud*, ed. James Strachey (London: Hogarth Press, 1953–74; originally published as a book preface, 1928), reprinted in *Dostoevsky: A Collection of Critical Essays*, ed. René Wellek (Englewood Cliffs, N.J.: Prentice-Hall, Inc., 1962), 103.

1. "Ku hai zhong de qiudu" ("Swimming Through the Sea of Bitterness") won a first-class prize for journalistic writing in 1994; published in Zhang Chenggong, *Zaolian weixian de kaiduan* (Beijing: Qunzhong Publishing Company, 1992). I am grateful to Emmanuel Sharef for locating a copy of this in China. The differences between the case and Yim Ho's film are many, and the fictionalization facilitates an appreciation of the filmmaker Yim Ho's psychological and ideological insertions. The names have all been changed. In real life, the father was not a school principal but an elementary school teacher from Santang Village; the mother was not an illiterate *doufu* maker but a well-educated seamstress; the woodcutter was a veterinarian; the grown son had become a government chauffeur in Beijing. While the son's warmer relationship to his kindly mother than to his rigidly stern father was an authentic feature of the original case, no hint of Oedipal conflict appears in the case report. The son, originally, brings his case not after long planning and research but through a chance encounter with a police captain, and he operates not out of sexual conflict but from a heightened sense of public obligation. The case is solved swiftly and without the dramatic tensions and narrative twists of Yim Ho's retelling. Whereas the journalist Zhang Chenggong (a former police officer himself) appears to be a straightforward spokesman for law and order, the psychological subtleties and political potential of the film derive primarily from Yim Ho's own creative imagination. "*Ku hai*, the sea of bitterness," is an ancient Chinese expression; in Daoist belief, it had to be crossed with the help of the Deity of Water in order to attain salvation from one's sins in this world of suffering. See Susan Huang, "Summoning the Gods: Paintings of Three Officials of Heaven, Earth and Water and Their Association with Daoist Ritual Performance in the Southern Song Period (1127–1279)," *Artibus Asiae* 61, no. 1 (2001): 5–52, especially 41 ff. In this regard it should be noted that in the original case, as recounted directly to author Zhang by the son, the mother repents deeply of her crime, in contrast to the film, where instead she remains resentful of the situation which led her to its commission.

In addition to this volume of legal cases, Zhang Chenggong later published a set of criminal cases from the city of Neijiang in the 1990s, *Tianfu zhi guo mo yu dao* (Criminals and justice in Sichuan province) (Beijing: Qunzhong Publishing Company, 1998).

2. For a study of Oedipal theory applied to early twentieth-century Chinese literature, see Jingyuan Zhang, *Psychoanalysis in China: Literary Transformations, 1919–1949* (Ithaca: East Asia Program, Cornell University, 1992), 68–84.

3. Freud, "Dostoevsky and Parricide," 103.

4. Cao Xueqin, translated by David Hawkes, *The Story of the Stone* [*The Dream of the Red Chamber*] (Harmondsworth: Penguin, 1978–86), 2:149.

5. Edwards, *Men and Women in Qing China*, 123.

6. Wolf, "Child Training and the Chinese Family," 40–41, 43.

7. Ibid., 47.

8. Ibid., 43.

9. While Guan Jian's abnormality derives from his mother's transgressiveness, her presence throughout the film remains too opaque, too obscure biographically to comprehend in any comparable psychological depth.

10. Wang, "*Red Sorghum:* Mixing Memory and Desire," 81.

11. Ibid., 83.

12. I write here not as a Freudian or a partisan of any particular psychological views or theories but in response to the orientation of the film itself.

13. "The relation of a boy to his father is, as we say, an 'ambivalent' one. In addition to the hate which seeks to get rid of the father as a rival, a measure of tenderness for him is also habitually present. The two attitudes of mind combine to produce identification with the father; the boy wants to be in his father's place because he admires him and wants to be like him, and also because he wants to put him out of the way. . . . At a certain moment, the child comes to understand that an attempt to remove his father as a rival would be punished by him with castration. So from fear of castration—that is, in the interests of preserving his masculinity—he gives up his wish to possess his mother and get rid of his father. In so far as this wish remains in the unconscious it forms the basis of the sense of guilt. We believe that what we have here been describing are normal processes, the normal fate of the so-called 'Oedipus complex'. . . . [T]hen, under the threat to the boy's masculinity by castration, his inclination becomes strengthened to diverge in the direction of femininity, to put himself instead in his mother's place and take over her role as object of his father's love. But the fear of castration [as a female] makes *this* solution impossible as well. . . . Thus both impulses, hatred of the father and being in love with the father, undergo repression. . . . If the father was hard, violent, and cruel, the super-ego takes over those attributes from him and, in the relations between the ego and it, the passivity which was supposed to have been repressed is re-established. The super-ego has become sadistic, and the ego becomes masochistic—that is to say, at bottom passive in a feminine way. A great need for punishment develops in the ego, which in part offers itself as a victim to Fate, and in part finds satisfaction in ill-treatment by the super-ego (that is, in the sense of guilt). For every punishment is ultimately castration and, as such, a fulfillment of the old passive attitude towards the father. Even Fate is, in the last resort, only a later projection of the father." Freud, "Dostoevsky and Parricide," 103–4.

14. See Jean Laplanche, *Life and Death in Psychoanalysis* (Baltimore: Johns Hopkins University Press, 1976), 97–102, for a psychoanalytic discussion of aggression, sadomasochism, and Freud's famous 1919 essay "A Child Is Being Beaten."

15. Freud writes of Hamlet's ability "to do anything but take vengeance upon the man who did away with his father and has taken his father's place with his mother—the man who shows him in realization the repressed desires of his own childhood." *The Interpretation of Dreams*, 310.

16. William Shakespeare, *Hamlet*, in *Shakespeare: The Complete Works*, ed. G. B. Harrison (New York: Harcourt, Brace, and World, 1968), 894.

17. Ibid., 895.

18. Freud, "Dostoevsky and Parricide," 107.

19. Ibid.

20. James Legge, trans., *Li Chi [Li ji]*, vol. 2 (New Hyde Park, N.Y.: University Books, 1967; original publication date 1885), 229.

21. See chap. 1, n. 21.

22. See chap. 3, p. 111, for this topic.

23. Anonymous, *Magistrate Teng Settles the Case of Inheritance with Ghostly Cleverness*, in *Stories Old and New: A Ming Dynasty Collection*, compiled by Feng Menglong, trans. Shuhui Yang and Yunqin Yang (Seattle and London: University of Washington Press, 2000), 172.

24. Jianying Zha, *China Pop: How Soap Operas, Tabloids, and Bestsellers Are Transforming a Culture* (New York: The New Press, 1995), 18.

25. This modern jurisprudence can be contrasted with that in *Judou*, another film featuring parental infidelity, a child trapped between warring parents, and parricide. In *Judou* the conflicts are handled more traditionally, within the confines of family and clan: by Judou's nephew (and lover) Tianqing, who restrains her from poisoning her abusive husband; by the clan elders who, being suspicious of Judou's transgressive relationship with Tianqing, convene and order their separation; and by their bastard child, the brooding Tianbai, increasingly unbalanced by his uncertain patrimony and the attendant social rejection he endures, who finally strikes out and murders his own adulterous father. The original novella by Liu Heng, *Fuxi, fuxi*, unlike the film, lodged a sincere concern for achieving social justice in clan elders and even in Tianbai, who has often been critically conceived as a "bad seed" but who in the novel condemns his father's lack of morals ("Haven't you any decency!") yet refrains from seriously harming him. See Silbergeld, *China Into Film*, 282–88.

26. "[The] feelings of guilt arising from his intention of murdering his father . . . also determined his attitude in the two other spheres in which the father-relation is the decisive factor, his attitude towards the authority of the state and towards belief in God. . . . Dostoevsky's condemnation as a political prisoner was unjust and he must have known it, but he accepted the undeserved punishment at the hands of the Little Father, the Tsar, as a substitute for the punishment he deserved for his sin against the real father." Freud, "Dostoevsky and Parricide," 106. Freud's misperceptions of Dostoevsky's relationship with his father and its putative role in the onset of his epilepsy are thoroughly critiqued in Joseph Frank, "Freud's Case-History of Dostoevsky," *Times Literary Supplement*, July 18, 1975, reprinted in Joseph Frank, *Dostoevsky: The Seeds of Revolt, 1821–1849* (Princeton: Princeton University Press, 1976), 379–91.

27. Sigmund Freud, *Totem and Taboo*, trans. James Strachey (New York: W. W. Norton, 1950), 63–64.

28. Jacques Lacan, *The Four Fundamental Concepts of Psychoanalysis*, trans. Alan Sheridan (New York: W. W. Norton, 1981), 34.

29. Cf. Kam Louie, *Inheriting Tradition: Interpretations of the Classical Philosophers in Communist China, 1949–1966* (Hong Kong: Oxford University Press, 1986).

30. Tani Barlow, "Theorizing Woman: *Funü, Guojia, Jiating* (Chinese Woman, Chinese State, Chinese Family)," in *Body, Subject and Power in China*, ed. Angela Zito and Tani Barlow (Chicago: University of Chicago Press, 1994), 273 and 278, n. 1.

31. Laurence Schneider, *A Madman of Ch'u: The Chinese Myth of Loyalty and Dissent* (Berkeley: University of California Press, 1980), 200; see especially chap. 5, "A Touch of Class: Ch'ü Yüan in the People's Republic."

32. So many other films have been viewed in the context of this transfer of colonial authority without adequate justification that I concur with Jenny Lau's critique of this proliferation as "reductionistic" and with her admonition that "This '1997' reading for every contemporary film coming from Hong Kong ran the risk of reducing Hong Kong culture in general, and film in particular, to the narrow spheres of economics and politics." "Besides Fists and Blood: Hong Kong Comedy and Its Master of the Eighties," *Cinema Journal* 37, no. 2 (winter 1998): 21–22. See, however, Yim Ho and Tsui Hark's *King of Chess* (1989), which satirically juxta-

posed China's cultural backwardness against Taiwan's gung-ho modernization, and Yim's subsequent film, *The Sun Has Ears* (1995). In the latter, as in *The Day the Sun Turned Cold*, two men compete for the affection, or mere control, of a lovely woman—two men who serially possess the same wife. As a practical matter, the wife is gradually drawn away from her husband, conspicuously surnamed Hu ("barbarian" or foreigner), by a cruel bandit-turned-military-officer who, like the Communists, unites the competing militias and brings peace and unity to the region ("After today, we'll never fight among ourselves again. We will all take orders from Chief Pan. We'll let Chief Pan lead us straight to Beijing."), but who also takes hostages and massacres children. The wife is torn between repulsion by his excesses and attraction to his self-confident authority. Finally, Yim Ho indulges the audience in a "happy ending" in which the wife avenges the massacre and kills Chief Pan, but he then casts doubt on whether such a tale could ever take place, whether a mere wife could actually resist male authority in this way— "How could a woman cause so much chaos and trouble? . . . as if the sun could grow ears and hear." For discussions of Yim Ho's film *Homecoming* (1984) in the context of Hong Kong politics, see Li Cheuk-to, "Return of the Father: Hong Kong New Wave and Its Chinese Context in the 1980s," in *New Chinese Cinemas*, ed. Browne et al., 151–59, and Leo Lee, "Two Films from Hong Kong: Parody and Allegory," in ibid., 180–215.

33. Cf. Li, "Return of the Father," 151–59; Chiao, "The Distinct Taiwanese and Hong Kong Cinemas"; Stephen Teo, *Hong Kong Cinema: The Extra Dimensions* (London: British Film Institute, 1997); Bordwell, *Planet Hong Kong*.

34. Cf. Ackbar Abbas, "The Erotics of Disappointment," in *Wong Kar-wai*, ed. Jean-Marc Lalanne et al. (Paris: Editions Dis Voir, n.d.), 39–81.

35. In the historical case, the mother's name was Deng Chuanxiu.

36. Teo, *Hong Kong Cinema*, 250.

37. Freud, "Dostoevsky and Parricide," 103.

38. Creon, it might be remembered, was not only Jocasta's brother but her husband Laius' uncle, sharing with Laius the male descent from Cadmus.

3. The Chinese Heart in Conflict with Itself: *Good Men, Good Women*

Epigraphs: Feodor Dostoevsky, *The Double*, in *Three Short Novels of Dostoevsky*, trans. Constance Garnett (Garden City, N.J.: Doubleday Anchor, 1960), 8; William Faulkner, *The Sound and the Fury* (1929; reprint, ed. David Minter, New York: W. W. Norton, 1994), 54.

1. Lan Bow-Chow, *Huangmache zhi ge* (Taipei: Shibao wenhua chubanshe, 1991). While listed in the film as providing the "original story," Lan's publication simply furnished some of the raw historical material for this complex dramatic rendering.

2. William Faulkner, *Requiem for a Nun* (1931; reprint, New York: Signet Books, 1954), 229.

3. *New York Times*, March 3, 2002, D7.

4. John Robert Shepherd, *Statecraft and Political Economy on the Taiwan Frontier, 1600–1800* (Stanford: Stanford University Press, 1993), 47.

5. As with Taiwan's identity, the identities of "China" and the fabrication of its so-called "Han" ethnic majority are the increasingly contested subject of a rapidly growing body of publications. See, for example, Frank Dikötter, *The Discourse of Race in Modern China* (Stanford: Stanford University Press, 1992); Lowell Ditmer and Samuel Kim, eds., *China's Quest for a National Identity* (Ithaca: Cornell University Press, 1993); Edward Friedman, "Reconstructing China's National Identity: A Southern Alternative to Mao-Era Anti-Imperialist Nationalism,"

Journal of Asian Studies 53, no. 1 (February 1994): 67–91; Dru Gladney, "Representing Nationality in China: Refiguring Majority/Minority Identities," *Journal of Asian Studies* 53, no.1 (February 1994): 92–123; Stevan Harrell, ed., *Cultural Encounters on China's Ethnic Frontiers* (Seattle: University of Washington Press, 1995); Prasenjit Duara, *Rescuing History from the Nation: Questioning Narratives of Modern China* (Chicago: University of Chicago Press, 1995); Laura Hostetler, *Qing Colonial Enterprise: Ethnography and Cartography in Early Modern China* (Chicago: University of Chicago Press, 2001); Clare Harris, *In the Image of Tibet: Tibetan Painting After 1959* (London: Reaktion Books, 1999).

6. In the scene rehearsing her liaison with Chung Hao-Tung.

7. Discussing her marriage to Chung Hao-Tung with her father.

8. A composite character in her own right, pop singer-actress Annie Shizuka Inoh, who plays Chiang Bi-Yu, was born in Taiwan in 1969 but has lived in Hong Kong and spent six teenage years in Japan; she speaks Taiwanese, Cantonese, Japanese, Mandarin, and English.

9. James Mottram, *The Making of Memento* (London: Faber and Faber, 2002).

10. Slavoj Žižek, *The Art of the Ridiculous Sublime: On David Lynch's Lost Highway*, introduction by Marek Wieczorek (Seattle: Walter Chapin Simpson Center for the Humanities and University of Washington Press, 2000).

11. *Psycho* was released both with and without the skull superimposed over Norman's face. There is also a doubling of explanations: the stilted artificiality of analytic *logic* in the next-to-last scene contrasted with the inner *experience* of Norman Bates in the last; see Slavoj Žižek on Hitchcock's multiple endings, "Why Is *Reality* Always Multiple?" in Žižek, *Enjoy Your Symptom!* 204 ff.

12. Fredric Jameson, "Remapping Taipei," in *New Chinese Cinemas*, ed. Browne et al., 117–50.

13. Cf. William Rothman, "*The Goddess:* Reflections on Melodrama East and West," in *Melodrama and Asian Cinema*, ed. Dissanayaki, 59–72.

14. Silbergeld, *China into Film*, chap. 3.

15. Lilian Lee, *Farewell My Concubine*, trans. Andrea Lingenfelter (New York: William Morrow, 1992), 2.

16. Translation by Yomi Braester, "Memory at a Standstill: 'Street-Smart History' in Jiang Wen's *In the Heat of the Sun*," *Screen*, 42, no. 4 (winter 2001): 352–53, 355; also, Yomi Braester, *Witness Against History* (Palo Alto: Stanford University Press, 2003), 196, 198.

17. Miklós Haraszti, *The Velvet Prison: Artists under State Socialism* (New York: New Republic/Basic Books, 1987), 121, 124.

18. See Wu Hung, *The Double Screen: Medium and Representation in Chinese Painting* (Chicago: University of Chicago Press and Reaktion Books, 1996).

19. Ibid., 231 ff. and fig. 163.

20. This has already been suggested by James Cahill, *Hills Beyond a River: Chinese Painting of the Yüan Dynasty, 1279–1368* (New York: Weatherhill, 1976), 116.

21. Ibid., fig. 66.

22. On the history and changing taxonomy of Chinese characterology, see Nanxiu Qian, *Spirit and Self in Medieval China: The Shih-shuo hsin-yü and Its Legacy* (Honolulu: University of Hawai'i Press, 2001).

23. Feodor Dostoevsky, letter dated October 1847, in Frank, *Dostoevsky: The Seeds of Revolt*, 296.

24. Dostoevsky, *The Double*, 8.

25. Ibid., 48.

26. Cf. Frank, *Dostoevsky: The Seeds of Revolt*, 296–99. Frank also cites studies of E. T. A. Hoffmann as a literary source for Dostoevsky's "device of the Doppelgänger" (298, n. 5).

27. See Faulkner, *Essays, Speeches, and Public Letters*, 119–20.

28. Dmitri Chizhevsky, "The Theme of the Double in Dostoevsky," trans. René Wellek, in *Dostoevsky*, ed. Wellek, 122.

29. Robert Yee-sin Chi, "Picture Perfect: Narrating Public Memory in Twentieth-Century China" (Ph.D. dissertation, Harvard University, 2001), 280–81, identifies Ozu's film in *Good Men, Good Women*, providing one additional ironic note: ". . . especially in light of previous comments by Hou to the effect that he developed his style long before he had seen any of Ozu's films [from which Hou's style has sometimes been declared to derive], it slyly and 'merely' confirms those early and imprecise comparisons" (281). For an excellent technical analysis of Hou's cinematic style in films through 1993 (before the production of *Good Men, Good Women*), arguing their significant difference from Ozu's films, see Shiao-ying Shen, "Permutations of the Foreigner: A Study of the Works of Edward Yang, Stan Lai, Chang Yi, and Hou Hsiao-hsien" (Ph.D. dissertation, Cornell University, 1995), 203–21.

30. My thanks to Marek Wieczorek for confirming Rossellini's identity and identifying this film for me.

31. Liang Ching seems to step right out of the descriptive first sentence of Freud's essay "On Narcissism: An Introduction": "a person who treats his [*sic*] own body in the same way in which the body of a sexual object is ordinarily treated—who looks at it, that is to say, strokes it and fondles it till he obtains complete satisfaction through these activities." Joseph Sandler, ed., *Freud's "On Narcissism: An Introduction"* (New Haven: Yale University Press, 1991), 3.

32. R. H. Mathews, *Mathews' Chinese-English Dictionary* (Shanghai: China Inland Mission and Presbyterian Mission Press, 1931), 116.

33. The Daoist associations of the mirror with the pursuit of *zhen*—truth or spiritual perfection—and magical revelation dates back to the early centuries B.C.E. For extensive consideration of this topic in an early Chinese context, see Eugene Wang, "Mirror, Death, and Rhetoric: Reading Later Han Chinese Bronze Artifacts," *Art Bulletin* 76, no. 3 (September 1994): 511–34; see also Lan-ying Tseng, "Picturing Heaven: Image and Knowledge in Han China" (Ph.D. dissertation, Harvard University, 2001), 42 ff.

34. Jacqueline Rose, in Jacques Lacan, *Feminine Sexuality: Jacques Lacan and the école freudienne*, trans. Jacqueline Rose, ed. Juliet Mitchell and Jacqueline Rose (New York: W. W. Norton, 1985), 30.

35. See Laplanche, *Life and Death in Psychoanalysis*, 97 ff., for a discussion of autoeroticism and its relationship to "introjecting the suffering object, fantasizing the suffering object, making the object suffer inside oneself, [and] making oneself suffer."

36. In his film diary, Hou records receiving the news from Taiwan of Chiang Bi-Yu's death on January 10, 1995. On the last page of these film notes, Hou records a day of "chilling winds and bitter rains" when he attended Chiang Bi-Yu's funeral ceremony together with a "host of the old classmates from her Mutual Assistance Society, who through these many years had entirely paled and disappeared from memory." In Chu T'ien-wen, ed., *Hao nan hao nü: Hou Hsiao-hsien paipian biji, fenchang, fenjing juben* (Taipei: Maitian chubanshe, 1995), 183, 188.

37. Jan Potocki, *The Manuscript Found in Saragossa*, trans. Ian MacLean (Middlesex, England: Penguin, 1996); translator's introduction, xiv. Filmed as *The Saragossa Manuscript*.

38. Ibid., i.

39. According to Faulkner, "[Color] would have cost so much, the editor couldn't undertake it." Frederick Gwynn and Joseph Blotner, eds., *Faulkner in the University: Class Conferences at the University of Virginia, 1957–1958* (New York: Vintage Books, 1965), 94.

40. A mere 3,300 copies of *The Sound and the Fury* were sold in the first fifteen years after publication, and not one of Faulkner's seventeen published novels remained in print in 1945,

five years before he received the Nobel Prize; cf. William Faulkner, *The Portable Faulkner*, ed. Malcom Cowley (New York: Vintage Books, 1954), 4. The novel was filmed in 1959 at Twentieth Century-Fox and directed by Martin Ritt. The screenplay was by Irving Ravetch and Harriet Frank, Jr., and the cast included Jack Warden (as Benjy), Margaret Leighton (Caddy), Joanne Woodward (Miss Quentin), Yul Brynner (Jason Jr.), and Ethel Waters (Dilsey).

41. Robert Chi writes of *Good Men, Good Women*'s "radically defamiliarizing techniques including chronological, performance, and audio/visual ones" leaving his audience "puzzled rather than enlightened, numb rather than engaged," and he contrasts this with the somewhat better received film on the same subject, *Super Citizen Ko* (director Wan Ren, 1995). Chi argues that Hou's audience "had come to expect a certain kind of film from Hou—based on a certain stable notion of his style." Chi, "Picture Perfect," 287–88. Hou Hsiao-hsien's scriptwriter, Chu T'ien-wen, similarly speaks of it as a major stylistic departure, but it is also true that the use of chronological sequences broken by narrative memory and flashbacks in Hou's well-received *The Puppetmaster*, which immediately preceded the film, reveals an evolution in style that led to that of *Good Men, Good Women;* Chu T'ien-wen, "Jeici kaishi dongle: tanlun *Hao nan, hao nü*" (This time [the camera] begins to move: Discussing *Good Men, Good Women*), in Chu, *Hao nan hao nü*, 8–13.

42. Jean-Paul Sartre, "Time in the Work of Faulkner," trans. Anette Michelson, in William Faulkner, *The Sound and the Fury* (1929; reprint, ed. David Minter, New York: W. W. Norton, 1994), 265.

43. Faulkner, *The Sound and the Fury*, 54.

44. The *New York Times* reacted to the announcement of Faulkner's Nobel Prize with hostility toward its rewarding the creation of "a society that is too often vicious, depraved, decadent, corrupt." Closer to home but from the opposite side of the political spectrum, the virulently racist Jackson *Daily News* wrote that "those who award the Nobel Prize are now laboring under the delusion that a novel, in order to be excellent, must also be nasty . . . he is a propagandist of degradation and properly belongs in the privy school of literature." Joseph Blottner, *Faulkner: A Biography*, vol. 2 (New York: Random House, 1974), 1344.

45. William Faulkner, *Absalom, Absalom!* (1936; reprint, New York: Random House, 1951), 378.

46. Although the English subtitles use the term "blood money," the film refers only to "money" and never clarifies what Liang Ching was paid for. However, the pre-shooting scenario indicates this was intended as hush money, paid for Liang Ching's false testimony that Ah Wei was armed and by implication threatening at the time of his shooting. Chu, *Hao nan hao nü*, 64.

47. After a long search, the real Chiang Bi-Yu was finally reunited with this son and with his son, her grandson, in 1990 in Guangdong province, as pictured in Lan, *Huangmache zhi ge*, photograph on first unpaginated photo page.

48. Chu, *Hao nan hao nü*, 7.

49. Ibid., 168 (italics added).

50. *HHH: Portrait de Hou Hsiao-Hsien* [*Cinema de notre temps: Hou Hsiao Hsien*] (1997), directed by Olivier Assayas, distributed by Les Films de l'Atalante.

51. Chu, *Hao nan hao nü*, 8–14.

52. Faulkner, *Faulkner in the University*, 31–32, 84, 87.

53. June Yip, "Constructing a Nation: Taiwanese History and the Films of Hou Hsiao-hsien," in *Transnational Chinese Cinemas*, ed. Lu, 139–68.

54. See Chi, "Picture Perfect," chap. 5. Chi notes the attention brought to the White Terror era by the discovery in 1993 in Taipei of the forgotten graves of 202 victims of the movement

(278), but he also writes about the greater reluctance of both the government and the populace in Taiwan to deal with this phenomenon as opposed to the February 28 Incident (263–66).

55. Chu, *Hao nan hao nü*, 14.

56. Ibid., 13–16. Others have claimed that Hou's interest in Annie Shizuka Inoh was provoked by criticism about his disregard for the role of women in earlier films. Cf. Mi Zou, "Nüren wu fa jinru lishi," in *Xin dianying zhi si*, ed. Mi Zou and Liang Xinhua (Taipei: T'ang-shan, 1991); Ye Yueyu, "Nüren jenda wu fa jinru lishi ma?" *Dangdai*, September 1994, 64–84.

57. Chi, "Picture Perfect," 76–80. Chi also reacts to Mi Zou's feminist critique, writing that "*Good Men, Good Women* responds by showing that not only can women enter history, they cannot escape it," 285.

58. Hou's father moved to Taichung in 1947 as executive secretary for the city mayor of Taichung. In 1948, he decided to stay on longer and had his family join him; in 1949 he was transferred to Taipei as commissioner of education.

59. Edward Yang, whose films, like *The Terrorizer*, often deal with or brush up against the criminal side of Taiwan life, has written that "The Taiwanese economy is about 40% an underground economy. If this situation isn't corrected, then I would say the government is similar to a mob." In Shelly Kraicer and Lisa Roosen-Runge, "Edward Yang: A Taiwanese Independent Filmmaker in Conversation," *Cineaction* 47 (September 1998): 53; quoted in Yingjin Zhang, *Screening China*, 304.

60. "If it had not been for these things, I might have lived out my life talking at street corners to scorning men. I might have died, unmarked, unknown, a failure. Now we are not a failure. This is our career and our triumph. Never in our full life could we hope to do such work for tolerance, for justice, for man's understanding of man as we now do by accident. Our words—our lives—our pains—nothing! The taking of our lives—lives of a good shoemaker [Nicola Sacco] and a poor fish-peddlar [Vanzetti]—all! That last moment belongs to us—that agony is our triumph." As reported by journalist Philip Strong, May 1927; in Nicola Sacco and Bartolomeo Vanzetti, *The Letters of Sacco and Vanzetti*, ed. Marion Denman Frankfurter and Gardner Jackson (New York: Penguin, 1997), lv.

61. Shiao-ying Shen has calculated the average length of shots in Hou's previous films: chronologically arranged, *Summer at Grandpa's*, 18 seconds per shot; *A Time to Live and a Time to Die*, 25 seconds per shot; *Dust in the Wind*, 32 seconds per shot; *Daughter of the Nile*, 27 seconds per shot; *A City of Sadness*, 44 seconds per shot; *The Puppetmaster*, 84 seconds per shot. She notes that Edward Yang's *The Terrorizer* contains 455 shots (20 seconds per shot) and quotes David Bordwell to the effect that Hollywood films average between 7 and 4.5 seconds per shot, while Soviet films of the 1920s might average as little as 2.4 seconds per shot. Shen, "Permutations of the Foreigner," 211–12. Calculations similar to Shen's are given in James Udden, "Hou Hsiao-hsien and the Question of a Chinese Cinema Style," *Asian Cinema* 13 (fall/winter 2002): 62. Udden provides a fine characterization of Hou's evolving style (*Good Men, Good Women* comes in for only one reference) while arguing persuasively against essentializing this personal style as "Chinese" ("Unfortunately, neither Hou Hsiao-hsien, nor the culture from which he arose, are that simple" [54]).

62. Interview in [Peggy] Hsiung-ping Chiao, "History's Subtle Shadows: Hou Hsiao-Hsien's *The Puppet Master*," *Cinemaya* 21 (1993): 7–8.

63. Ibid., 7.

64. Ibid., 9–10.

65. Ryunosuke Akutagawa, *Rashomon and Other Stories*, trans. Takashi Kojima (Tokyo: Hara Shobo, 1964).

66. Shen, "Permutations of the Foreigner," 205–9.

67. Ibid., 191–92.

68. Cf. Judith Shapiro, *Mao's War Against Nature: Politics and the Environment in Revolutionary China* (New York: Cambridge University Press, 2001).

69. Ah Cheng, *King of the Trees*, in Ah Cheng, *Three Kings*, trans. Bonnie McDougall (London: Collins Harvill, 1990), 110–11 (my italics).

70. Ibid., 108.

71. Ibid., 153. The companion pieces in this trilogy, translated in the same volume, are Ah Cheng's *King of the Children*, made into a film by director Chen Kaige and cinematographer Gu Changwei (1987), and *King of Chess*, directed in film by Yim Ho and Tsui Hark and co-produced by Tsui Hark and Hou Hsiao-hsien (1989). *King of the Trees*, sadly, has never been made into film. Perhaps Hou Hsiao-hsien, who is friends with Ah Cheng, might do it someday.

72. Anonymous, *Magistrate Teng Settles the Case*, 172 (italics added).

73. Kiyohiko Munakata, *Ching Hao's Pi-fa-chi: A Note on the Art of the Brush* (Ascona: Artibus Asiae, 1975), 11, 13–14, 16.

74. Richard Barnhart, *Wintry Forests, Old Trees: Some Landscape Themes in Chinese Painting* (New York: China Institute in America, 1972).

75. Robert Maeda, *Two Twelfth Century Texts on Chinese Painting* (Ann Arbor: University of Michigan Center for Chinese Studies, 1970), 57.

76. Robert Hans van Gulik, *The Gibbon in China: An Essay in Animal Lore* (Leiden: E. J. Brill, 1967).

77. With the film script comes the note, "It is not clear if they are crying or laughing." Chu, *Hao nan hao nü*, 121.

78. Shi Nai'an (attributed), *The Water-Margin* (Shuihu zhuan), translated by Pearl Buck as *All Men Are Brothers*, 19.

BIBLIOGRAPHY

ABBAS, ACKBAR. "The Erotics of Disappointment." In *Wong Kar-wai*, ed. Jean-Marc Lalanne et al. Paris: Editions Dis Voir, n.d.

AH CHENG. *King of the Trees*. In Ah Cheng, *Three Kings*, trans. Bonnie McDougall. London: Collins Harvill, 1990.

ANDERSEN, HANS CHRISTIAN. "The Little Mermaid." In *Tales and Stories by Hans Christian Andersen*, trans. Pat Conroy and Sven Rossel. Seattle: University of Washington Press, 1980.

AUILER, DAN. *Vertigo: The Making of a Hitchcock Classic*. New York: St. Martin's Press, 1998.

BARLOW, TANI. "Theorizing Woman: *Funü, Guojia, Jiating* (Chinese Woman, Chinese State, Chinese Family)." In *Body, Subject and Power in China*, ed. Angela Zito and Tani Barlow. Chicago: University of Chicago Press, 1994.

BARNHART, RICHARD. *Wintry Forests, Old Trees: Some Landscape Themes in Chinese Painting*. New York: China Institute in America, 1972.

BARR, CHARLES. *Vertigo*. London: British Film Institute, 2002.

BERMAN, EMANUEL. "Hitchcock's *Vertigo:* The Collapse of a Rescue Fantasy." In *Psychoanalysis and Film*, ed. Glen Gabbard. London: Karnac, 2001.

BERRY, CHRIS. "The Sublimitive Text: Sex and Revolution in *Big Road*." *East-West Film Journal* 2, no. 2 (1988).

BLOTTNER, JOSEPH. *Faulkner: A Biography*. 2 vols. New York: Random House, 1974.

BORDWELL, DAVID. *Narration in the Fiction Film*. Madison: University of Wisconsin Press, 1985.

———. *Planet Hong Kong: Popular Cinema and the Art of Entertainment*. Cambridge: Harvard University Press, 2000.

BRAESTER, YOMI. "Memory at a Standstill: 'Street-Smart History' in Jiang Wen's *In the Heat of the Sun*." *Screen* 42, no. 4 (winter 2001): 350–62.

———. *Witness Against History: Literature, Film, and Public Discourse in Twentieth-Century China*. Palo Alto: Stanford University Press, 2003.

BROWNE, NICK. "Society and Objectivity: On the Political Economy of Chinese Melodrama." In *New Chinese Cinemas: Forms, Identities, Politics*, ed. Nick Browne et al. New York: Cambridge University Press, 1994.

CAO XUEQIN. *The Story of the Stone* [*The Dream of the Red Chamber*]. 6 vols. Trans. David Hawkes. Harmondsworth: Penguin, 1978–86.

CAO ZHI [TS'AO CHIH]. "The Goddess of the Luo." In *Chinese Rhyme-Prose: Poems from the Chinese in Fu Form from the Han and Six Dynasties Periods*, trans. David Hawkes. New York: Columbia University Press, 1971.

CHANG, MICHAEL. "The Good, the Bad, and the Beautiful: Movie Actresses and Public Discourse in Shanghai, 1920s–1930s." In *Cinema and Urban Culture in Shanghai, 1922–1943*, ed. Yingjin Zhang. Stanford: Stanford University Press, 2002.

CHI, ROBERT YEE-SIN. "Picture Perfect: Narrating Public Memory in Twentieth-Century China." Ph.D. dissertation, Harvard University, 2001.

CHIAO, [PEGGY] HSIUNG-PING. "Hou Hsiao-hsien's Rocky Road to the Golden Lion." *Sinorama*, November 1989.

———. "The Distinct Taiwanese and Hong Kong Cinemas." In *Perspectives on Chinese Cinema*, ed. Chris Berry. 2nd ed. London: British Film Institute, 1991.

———. "History's Subtle Shadows: Hou Hsiao-Hsien's *The Puppet Master*." *Cinemaya* 21 (1993).

CHIZHEVSKY, DMITRI. "The Theme of the Double in Dostoevsky." Trans. René Wellek. In *Dostoevsky: A Collection of Critical Essays*, ed. René Wellek. Englewood Cliffs, N.J.: Prentice-Hall, Inc., 1962.

CHOW, REY. *Primitive Passions: Visuality, Sexuality, Ethnography, and Contemporary Chinese Cinema*. New York: Columbia University Press, 1995.

CHU T'IEN-WEN, ed. *Hao nan hao nü: Hou Hsiao-hsien paipian biji, fenchang, fenjing juben* (*Good Men, Good Women:* Hou Hsiao-hsien's filming notes, screenplay, and film script). Taipei: Maitian chubanshe, 1995.

CLARK, PAUL. "The Sinification of Cinema: The Foreignness of Film in China." In *Cinema and Cultural Identity: Reflections on Films from Japan, India, and China*, ed. Wimal Dissanayake. Lanham, Md.: University Press of America, 1988.

The Classic of Filial Piety [Xiao jing]. Trans. James Legge as *Hsiao King*. In *The Sacred Books of China: The Texts of Confucianism*. 4 vols. Oxford: Oxford University Press, 1879.

COWLEY, MALCOLM, ed. *The Portable Faulkner*. New York: Vintage Books, 1954.

CUI, SHUQIN. "Gendered Perspective: The Construction and Representation of Subjectivity and Sexuality in *Ju Dou*." In *Transnational Chinese Cinemas: Identity, Nationhood, Gender*, ed. Sheldon Lu. Honolulu: University of Hawai'i Press, 1997.

DIKOTTER, FRANK. *The Discourse of Race in Modern China*. Stanford: Stanford University Press, 1992.

DISSANAYAKE, WIMAL, ed. *Cinema and Cultural Identity: Reflections on Films from Japan, India, and China*. Lanham, Md.: University Press of America, 1988.

———. *Melodrama and Asian Cinema*. New York: Cambridge University Press, 1993.

DITMER, LOWELL, AND SAMUEL KIM, eds. *China's Quest for a National Identity*. Ithaca: Cornell University Press, 1993.

DOSTOEVSKY, FEODOR. *The Double*. In *Three Short Novels of Dostoevsky*, trans. Constance Garnett. Garden City, N.J.: Doubleday Anchor, 1960.

DUARA, PRASENJIT. *Rescuing History from the Nation: Questioning Narratives of Modern China*. Chicago: University of Chicago Press, 1995.

EDWARDS, LOUISE. *Men and Women in Qing China: Gender in The Red Chamber Dream*. Honolulu: University of Hawai'i Press, 1994.

EHRLICH, LINDA, AND DAVID DESSER, eds. *Cinematic Landscapes: Observations on the Visual Arts and Cinema of China and Japan*. Austin: University of Texas Press, 1994.

ELLICKSON, LEE. "Preparing to Live in the Present: An Interview with Hou Hsiao-hsien." *Cineaste* 27, no. 4 (fall 2002).

FAULKNER, WILLIAM. *Absalom, Absalom!* 1936. Reprint, New York: Random House, 1951.

———. *The Portable Faulkner*. Ed. Malcolm Cowley. New York: Vintage Books, 1954.

———. *Requiem for a Nun*. 1931. Reprint, New York: Signet Books, 1954.

———. *The Sound and the Fury*. 1929. Reprint, ed. David Minter, New York: W. W. Norton, 1994.

FENG MENGLONG, comp. *Stories Old and New: A Ming Dynasty Collection*. Seattle and London, University of Washington Press, 2000.

FONG, WEN. "The Problem of Forgeries in Chinese Painting." *Artibus Asiae* 25 (1962).

FRANK, JOSEPH. *Dostoevsky: The Seeds of Revolt, 1821–1849*. Princeton: Princeton University Press, 1976.

———. *Dostoevsky: The Years of Ordeal, 1850–1859*. Princeton: Princeton University Press, 1983.

FREUD, SIGMUND. *The Interpretation of Dreams*. In *The Basic Writings of Sigmund Freud*, trans. A. A. Brill. New York: Random House, 1938 (originally published 1900).

———. *Totem and Taboo*. Trans. James Strachey. New York: W. W. Norton, 1950.

———. *Civilization and Its Discontents*. Trans. James Strachey. New York: W. W. Norton, 1961.

———. "Dostoevsky and Parricide." Trans. D. F. Tait. In *Standard Edition of the Collected Psychological Works of Sigmund Freud*, ed. James Strachey. London: Hogarth Press, 1953–74 (originally published as a book preface, 1928). Reprinted in *Dostoevsky: A Collection of Critical Essays*, ed. René Wellek. Englewood Cliffs, N.J.: Prentice-Hall, Inc., 1962.

FRIEDMAN, EDWARD. "Reconstructing China's National Identity: A Southern Alternative to Mao-Era Anti-Imperialist Nationalism." *Journal of Asian Studies* 53, no. 1 (February 1994).

GABBARD, GLEN, ed. *Psychoanalysis and Film*. London: Karnac, 2001.

GABBARD, GLEN, AND KRIN GABBARD. *Psychiatry and the Cinema*. 2nd ed. Washington, D.C.: American Psychiatric Press, 1999.

GLADNEY, DRU. "Representing Nationality in China: Refiguring Majority/Minority Identities." *Journal of Asian Studies* 53, no.1 (February 1994).

GREENBERG, JONAH. "Voyeur Eyes Only: Lou Ye's Variations on Romance." *Virtual China*, 1999: <www.virtualchina.com>

GULIK, ROBERT HANS VAN. *The Gibbon in China: An Essay in Animal Lore*. Leiden: E. J. Brill, 1967.

GWYNN, FREDERICK, AND JOSEPH BLOTNER, eds. *Faulkner in the University: Class Conferences at the University of Virginia, 1957–1958*. New York: Vintage Books, 1965.

HARASZTI, MIKLÓS. *The Velvet Prison: Artists under State Socialism*. New York: New Republic/ Basic Books, 1987.

HARRELL, STEVAN, ed. *Cultural Encounters on China's Ethnic Frontiers*. Seattle: University of Washington Press, 1995.

HOSTETLER, LAURA. *Qing Colonial Enterprise: Ethnography and Cartography in Early Modern China*. Chicago: University of Chicago Press, 2001.

HUANG SHIXIAN. "Zhongguo 'hunian'" (Chinese year of the tiger). In *Dangdai Zhongguo dianying: 1998* (Contemporary Chinese cinema: 1998). Taipei: Shibao wenhua, 1999.

ING, DAVID. "Love at Last Site: Waiting for Oedipus in Stanley Kwan's *Rouge*." *Camera Obscura* 32 (1993–94).

JAMESON, FREDRIC. "Remapping Taipei." In *New Chinese Cinemas: Forms, Identities, Politics*, ed. Nick Browne et al. New York: Cambridge University Press, 1994.

KAPLAN, E. ANN. "Problematizing Cross-Cultural Analysis: The Case of Women in the Recent Chinese Cinema." In *Perspectives on Chinese Cinema*, ed. Chris Berry. 2nd ed. London: British Film Institute, 1991. First published in *Wide Angle* 11, no. 2 (1989).

———. "Reading Formations and Chen Kaige's *Farewell My Concubine*." In *Transnational Chinese Cinemas: Identity, Nationhood, Gender*, ed. Sheldon Lu. Honolulu: University of Hawai'i Press, 1997.

KING, DAVID. *The Commissar Vanishes: The Falsification of Photographs and Art in Stalin's Russia*. New York: Metropolitan Books/Henry Holt and Company, 1997.

LACAN, JACQUES. *The Four Fundamental Concepts of Psychoanalysis*. Trans. Alan Sheridan. New York: W. W. Norton, 1981.

———. *Feminine Sexuality: Jacques Lacan and the école freudienne*. Trans. Jacqueline Rose, ed. Juliet Mitchell and Jacqueline Rose. New York: W. W. Norton, 1985.

LAN BOW-CHOW. *Huangmache zhi ge* (Song of the covered wagon). Taipei: Shibao wenhua chubanshe, 1991.

LAPLANCHE, JEAN. *Life and Death in Psychoanalysis*. Baltimore: Johns Hopkins University Press, 1976.

LAU, JENNY KWOK WAH. "A Cultural Interpretation of the Popular Cinema of China and Hong Kong." In *Perspectives on Chinese Cinema*, ed. Chris Berry. 2nd ed. London: British Film Institute, 1991.

———. "Besides Fists and Blood: Hong Kong Comedy and Its Master of the Eighties." *Cinema Journal* 37, no. 2 (winter 1998).

LEDDEROSE, LOTHAR. *Ten Thousand Things: Module and Mass Production in Chinese Art*. Princeton: Princeton University Press, 2000.

LEE, LEO. "Two Films from Hong Kong: Parody and Allegory." In *New Chinese Cinemas: Forms, Identities, Politics*, ed. Nick Browne et al. New York: Cambridge University Press, 1994.

———. *Shanghai Modern: The Flowering of a New Urban Culture in China, 1930*. Cambridge: Harvard University Press, 1999.

LEGGE, JAMES, trans. *Li Chi* [*Li ji*] (Book of rites). 4 vols. 1885. Reprint, New Hyde Park, N.Y.: University Books, 1967.

LEVY, RICHARD. "Corruption in Popular Culture." In *Popular China: Unofficial Culture in a Globalizing Society*, ed. Perry Link et al. Lanham, Md.: Rowman and Littlefield, 2002.

LI CHEUK-TO. "Return of the Father: Hong Kong New Wave and Its Chinese Context in the 1980s." In *New Chinese Cinemas: Forms, Identities, Politics*, ed. Nick Browne et al. New York: Cambridge University Press, 1994.

LIM, DENNIS. "Lou Ye's Generation Next." *Village Voice*, November 14, 2000.

LINK, PERRY, AND KATE ZHOU. "Shunkouliu: Popular Satirical Sayings and Popular Thought." In *Popular China: Unofficial Culture in a Globalizing Society*, ed. Perry Link et al. Lanham, Md.: Rowman and Littlefield, 2002.

LOUIE, KAM. *Inheriting Tradition: Interpretations of the Classical Philosophers in Communist China, 1949–1966*. Hong Kong: Oxford University Press, 1986.

LU, SHELDON, ed. *Transnational Chinese Cinemas: Identity, Nationhood, Gender*. Honolulu: University of Hawai'i Press, 1997.

LU, TONGLIN. *Confronting Modernity in the Cinemas of Taiwan and Mainland China*. New York: Cambridge University Press, 2002.

MA NING. "Spatiality and Subjectivity in Xie Jin's Film Melodrama of the New Period."
In *New Chinese Cinemas: Forms, Identities, Politics*, ed. Nick Browne et al. New York:
Cambridge University Press, 1994.

MI ZOU. "Nüren wu fa jinru lishi?" (Can't women enter history?). In *Xin dianying zhi si* (The
death of the new cinema), ed. Mi Zou and Liang Xinhua. Taipei: T'ang-shan, 1991.

MULVEY, LAURA. "Visual Pleasure and Narrative Cinema." *Screen* 16, no. 5 (autumn 1975).

MUNAKATA, KIYOHIKO. *Ching Hao's Pi-fa-chi: A Note on the Art of the Brush*. Ascona: Artibus
Asiae, 1975.

NANXIU QIAN. *Spirit and Self in Medieval China: The Shih-shuo hsin-yü and Its Legacy*. Honolulu: University of Hawai'i Press, 2001.

PERRY, ELIZABETH, AND LI XUN. *Proletarian Power: Shanghai in the Cultural Revolution*. Boulder:
Westview Press, 1997.

PICKOWICZ, PAUL. "Melodramatic Representation and the 'May Fourth' Tradition of Chinese
Cinema." In *From May Fourth to June Fourth: Fiction and Film in Twentieth-Century
China*, ed. Ellen Widmer and David Der-wei Wang. Cambridge: Harvard University
Press, 1993.

PICKOWICZ, PAUL, AND LIPING WANG. "Village Voices, Urban Activists: Women, Violence, and
Gender Inequality in Rural China." In *Popular China: Unofficial Culture in a Globalizing Society*, ed. Perry Link et al. Lanham, Md.: Rowman and Littlefield, 2002.

PORFIRO, ROBERT. "No Way Out: Existential Motifs in the *Film Noir*." In *Film Noir Reader*,
ed. Alain Silver and James Ursini. New York: Limelight Editions, 1996.

POTOCKI, JAN. *The Manuscript Found in Saragossa*. Trans. Ian MacLean. Middlesex,
England: Penguin, 1996.

ROTHMAN, WILLIAM. "*The Goddess:* Reflections on Melodrama East and West." In *Melodrama
and Asian Cinema*, ed. Wimal Dissanayake. New York: Cambridge University Press,
1993.

SANDLER, JOSEPH, ed. *Freud's "On Narcissism: An Introduction."* New Haven: Yale University
Press, 1991.

SARTRE, JEAN-PAUL. "Time in the Work of Faulkner." Trans. Anette Michelson. In William
Faulkner, *The Sound and the Fury*, 1929. Reprint, ed. David Minter, New York:
W. W. Norton, 1994.

SHAPIRO, JUDITH. *Mao's War Against Nature: Politics and the Environment in Revolutionary
China*. New York: Cambridge University Press, 2001.

SHEN, SHIAO-YING. "Permutations of the Foreigner: A Study of the Works of Edward Yang,
Stan Lai, Chang Yi, and Hou Hsiao-hsien." Ph.D. dissertation, Cornell University, 1995.

SHEPHERD, JOHN ROBERT. *Statecraft and Political Economy on the Taiwan Frontier, 1600–1800*.
Stanford: Stanford University Press, 1993.

SILBERGELD, JEROME. *China into Film: Frames of Reference in Contemporary Chinese Cinema*.
London: Reaktion Books, 1999.

SILBERGELD, JEROME, WITH GONG JISUI. *Contradictions: Artistic Life, the Socialist State, and the
Chinese Painter Li Huasheng*. Seattle and London: University of Washington Press, 1993.

SPOTO, DONALD. *The Art of Alfred Hitchcock: Fifty Years of His Motion Pictures*. 2nd ed. New
York: Anchor/Doubleday, 1992.

———. *The Dark Side of Genius: The Life of Alfred Hitchcock*. Boston: Little Brown, 1983.

STOKES, LISA ODHAM, AND MICHAEL HOOVER. *City on Fire: Hong Kong Cinema*. London: Verso, 1999.

TANG XIANZU [TANG HSIEN-TSU]. *The Peony Pavilion*. Trans. Cyril Birch. Bloomington: Indiana University Press, 1980.

TAY, WILLIAM. "The Ideology of Initiation: The Films of Hou Hsiao-hsien." In *New Chinese Cinemas: Forms, Identities, Politics*, ed. Nick Browne et al. New York: Cambridge University Press, 1994.

TEO, STEPHEN. *Hong Kong Cinema: The Extra Dimensions*. London: British Film Institute, 1997.

TRUFFAUT, FRANCOIS. *Hitchcock*. Rev. ed. New York: Simon and Schuster/Touchstone, 1985.

TSENG, LAN-YING. "Picturing Heaven: Image and Knowledge in Han China," Ph.D. dissertation, Harvard University, 2001.

UDDEN, JAMES. "Hou Hsiao-hsien and the Question of a Chinese Cinema Style." *Asian Cinema* 13 (fall/winter 2002).

WANG, YUEJIN [EUGENE]. "*Red Sorghum:* Mixing Memory and Desire." In *Perspectives on Chinese Cinema*, ed. Chris Berry. 2nd ed. London: British Film Institute, 1991.

———. "Mirror, Death, and Rhetoric: Reading Later Han Chinese Bronze Artifacts." *Art Bulletin* 76, no. 3 (September 1994).

WELLEK, RENÉ, ed. *Dostoevsky: A Collection of Critical Essays*. Englewood Cliffs, N.J.: Prentice-Hall, Inc., 1962.

WOLF, MARGERY. "Child Training and the Chinese Family." In *Family and Kinship in Chinese Society*, ed. Maurice Friedman. Stanford: Stanford University Press, 1970.

WU HUNG. *The Double Screen: Medium and Representation in Chinese Painting*. Chicago: University of Chicago Press and Reaktion Books, 1996.

XIAO JING. See *The Classic of Filial Piety*.

XIAO, ZHIWEI. "Anti-Imperialism and Film Censorship during the Nanjing Decade, 1927–1937." In *Transnational Chinese Cinemas: Identity, Nationhood, Gender*, ed. Sheldon Lu. Honolulu: University of Hawai'i Press, 1997.

———. "Constructing a New National Culture: Film Censorship and the Issues of Cantonese Dialect, Superstition, and Sex in the Nanjing Decade." In *Cinema and Urban Culture in Shanghai, 1922–1943*, ed. Yingjin Zhang. Stanford: Stanford University Press, 1999.

YANG, MAYFAIR. "Of Gender, State, Censorship, and Overseas Capital: An Interview with Chinese Director Zhang Yimou." *Public Culture* 5 (1993). Reprinted in *Zhang Yimou: Interviews*, ed. Frances Gateward. Jackson: University of Mississippi Press, 2001.

YANG, SHUHUI, AND YUNQIN YANG, trans. *Stories Old and New: A Ming Dynasty Collection Compiled by Feng Menglong*. Seattle and London: University of Washington Press, 2000.

YATSKO, PAMELA. *New Shanghai: The Rocky Rebirth of China's Legendary City*. New York: John Wiley and Sons, 2001.

YAU, ESTHER. "Border Crossing: Mainland China's Presence in Hong Kong Cinema." In *New Chinese Cinemas: Forms, Identities, Politics*, ed. Nick Browne et al. New York: Cambridge University Press, 1994.

———, ed. *At Full Speed: Hong Kong Cinema in a Borderless World*. Minneapolis: University of Minnesota Press, 2001.

YE YUEYU. "Nüren jenda wu fa jinru lishi ma?" (Can women *not* enter history?). *Dangdai*, September 1994.

YINGJIN ZHANG, ZHIWEI XIAO, ET AL. *Encyclopedia of Chinese Film*. London and New York: Routledge, 1998.

YIP, JUNE. "Constructing a Nation: Taiwanese History and the Films of Hou Hsiao-hsien." In *Transnational Chinese Cinemas: Identity, Nationhood, Gender*, ed. Sheldon Lu. Honolulu: University of Hawai'i Press, 1997.

YOUNG-BRUEHL, ELISABETH, ed. *Freud on Women: A Reader*. New York: W. W. Norton, 1990.

ZHA, JIANYING. *China Pop: How Soap Operas, Tabloids, and Bestsellers Are Transforming a Culture*. New York: The New Press, 1995.

ZHANG CHENGGONG. "Ku hai zhong de qiudu" (Swimming through the sea of bitterness). In Zhang Chenggong, *Zaolian weixian de kaiduan*. Beijing: Qunzhong Publishing Company, 1992.

ZHANG JINGYUAN. *Psychoanalysis in China: Literary Transformations, 1919–1949*. Ithaca: East Asia Program, Cornell University, 1992.

ZHANG JUNXIANG. "Essay Done in Film Terms." In *Chinese Film Theory: A Guide to the New Era*, ed. George Semsel, Xiao Hong, and Hou Jianping. New York: Praeger, 1990.

ZHANG, YINGJIN. "Prostitution and Urban Imagination: Negotiating the Public and the Private in Chinese Films of the 1930s." In *Cinema and Urban Culture in Shanghai, 1922–1943*, ed. Yingjin Zhang. Stanford: Stanford University Press, 1999.

———. *Screening China: Critical Interventions, Cinematic Transformations, and the Transnational Imaginary in Contemporary Chinese Cinema*. Ann Arbor: University of Michigan Center for Chinese Studies, 2002.

ZHANG JINGJIN, ed. *Cinema and Urban Culture in Shanghai, 1922–1943*. Stanford: Stanford University Press, 1999.

ŽIŽEK, SLAVOJ. *Looking Awry: An Introduction to Jacques Lacan through Popular Culture*. Cambridge, Mass.: MIT Press, 1991.

———. *The Art of the Ridiculous Sublime: On David Lynch's Lost Highway*. Introduction by Marek Wieczorek. Seattle: Walter Chapin Simpson Center for the Humanities and University of Washington Press, 2000.

———. *Enjoy Your Symptom! Jacques Lacan in Hollywood and Out*. Rev. ed. New York: Routledge, 2001.